Endorsements

Wise for Salvation has accomplished what few resources have been able to do: provide interactive devotions for young learners that are at the same time simple, interactive and faithful to scripture. Families (even those with not-so-young children) will enjoy these engaging activities designed to help them know God and his Word better, and the best part is that almost all of them can be done with items they already have on hand! Thank you, Christie, for this great resource!

Sean Anderson

Director, School of Children's and Family Ministry

Vanguard College, Edmonton, AB

Christie Thomas is one of the most creative children's ministry workers I know. She is passionately committed to kids and is convinced that children of any age can, and should, have a deeply meaningful relationship with God. As you journey through this book, with its readings and exercises, you will get a taste of Christie's creativity. She will ask you to explore each Bible story in terms a child can understand, and that will require, in some sense, that you become like a child yourself. If you take the adventure, you will watch your little one(s) growing in their love for Jesus, and I am sure you will find yourself growing in your love for Jesus as well.

Pastor Tom Baird

Bethel Community Church, Edmonton, AB

Wise for Salvation resonates with my convictions that God's Word is relevant and active in even the youngest. Christie has written devotions that are creative and interactive to capture kids' attentions and imaginations, taking kids and parents on a joy-filled journey of encountering God. I am excited to recommend this resource to young families.

Pastor Donna Hernandez

Children's Ministry Pastor

Sherwood Park Alliance Church, Sherwood Park, AB

After two weeks of trying out this new children's devotional by Christie Thomas, I'm happy to say that I have found our go-to daily devotional for our three younger children. I found this to be the perfect book for my 9-, 6- and 3-year-old children. My 9-year-old is able to look up, in her Bible, the verse we are studying for the week. Then either she or I can read it to her younger siblings. The daily activities are well planned and suited for multiple ages. I found them to be quick, fun, and very engaging. My busy 3- and 6-year-old are reminded of the story and concept through the activities all week long and my 9-year-old enjoys these as well. This mom's favorite part is that no one is bored or distracted! The reading and activities are the right length to keep kids interested and engaged and the questions help to give depth and perspective. The studies are formatted nicely with topics listed for choosing specifically or going through in order. We laugh and spend time together learning about our Savior. What could be better? I would definitely recommend this to my friends and family.

Michelle Drost

Mother of five

I wish I had this book when I was first looking for a preschool-aged devotional! Christie Thomas engages preschoolers with Bible stories at their level, without turning those stories into simple platitudes. Kids will enjoy these short encounters with God's story.

Christina Patterson
Mother of three boys

I would recommend that every parent read this devotional resource with their preschoolers. Christie's unique ability to connect with young children results in devotions that effectively encourage a daily walk with God, creatively teach Biblical truths, carefully help children focus on the needs of others, and successfully demonstrate how God influences each part of our day. Christie's devotions are packed with practical teaching ideas that can easily be adapted to any preschooler's learning style, and many parts of her book can be incorporated throughout a family's daily routine.

Christina Froehlich, BScN
Mother of five

Wise for Salvation is perfect for preschoolers because it helps them step into the Bible stories in very concrete ways, connecting them with tangible items mentioned in the stories and making the stories come alive. There are a variety of strategies for exploring each story, so children with various learning styles will be engaged. Children are always being pointed back to what God is doing in the story and what God is able to do in their own lives.

Jennifer Porritt
Mother of three

Simple and fun ways to apply God's word to my preschooler's life. When we were doing one activity my daughter exclaimed, "This is silly!" and then the next day as we were walking together the topic came up again and we had a very meaningful conversation. Best preschooler devotional book we've used!

Heather Spronk
Mother of two

Wise for Salvation

Meaningful Devotions for Families with Little Ones

Christie Thomas

Wise For Salvation
Copyright © 2015 by Christie Thomas

All rights reserved. Neither this publication nor any part of this publication may be reproduced or transmitted in any form or by any means, electronic or mechanical, including photocopying, recording or any information storage and retrieval system, without permission in writing from the author.

Scripture taken from the HOLY BIBLE, NEW INTERNATIONAL VERSION®. Copyright © 1973, 1978, 1984 International Bible Society. Used by permission of Zondervan. All rights

Scripture quotations marked (NIV) are taken from the HOLY BIBLE, NEW INTERNATIONAL VERSION®. NIV®. Copyright © 1973, 1978, 1984 by International Bible Society. Used by permission of Zondervan. All rights reserved.

Scripture taken from the New Century Version®. Copyright © 2005 by Thomas Nelson, Inc. Used by permission. All rights reserved.

The Holy Bible, English Standard Version (ESV) is adapted from the Revised Standard Version of the Bible, copyright Division of Christian Education of the National Council of the Churches of Christ in the U.S.A. All rights reserved.

ISBN: 978-1-4866-0849-2

Printed in Canada

Word Alive Press
131 Cordite Road, Winnipeg, MB R3W 1S1
www.wordalivepress.ca

Library and Archives Canada Cataloguing in Publication

Thomas, Christie, 1982-, author
    Wise for salvation : meaningful devotions for families with little ones / Christie Thomas.

Issued in print and electronic formats.
ISBN 978-1-4866-0849-2 (pbk.).--ISBN 978-1-4866-0850-8 (pdf).--
ISBN 978-1-4866-0851-5 (html).--ISBN 978-1-4866-0852-2 (epub)

     1. Families--Prayers and devotions.
     2. Children--Prayers and devotions.
     3. Families--Religious life. I. Title.

BV255.T55 2015   249   C2015-900281-8
                                               C2015-900282-6

To Ethan, Oliver, and Jackson

May you follow in the footsteps of Christ,

becoming wise for salvation.

May Christ make his home in your hearts as you trust in him.

May your roots grow down into God's love and keep you strong.

May you have the power to know, as all God's people should,

how wide, how long, how high, and how deep his love is.

May you experience the love of Christ,

though it is too great to understand fully.

May you be made complete with all the fullness

of life and power that comes from God.

Contents

Acknowledgements xi

Introduction.. xiii

Old Testament... 1

Christmas 91

The Life of Jesus 101

Jesus' Death, Resurrection, and Ascension 147

The Early Church 165

Loving and Listening to God... 185

Index.. 199

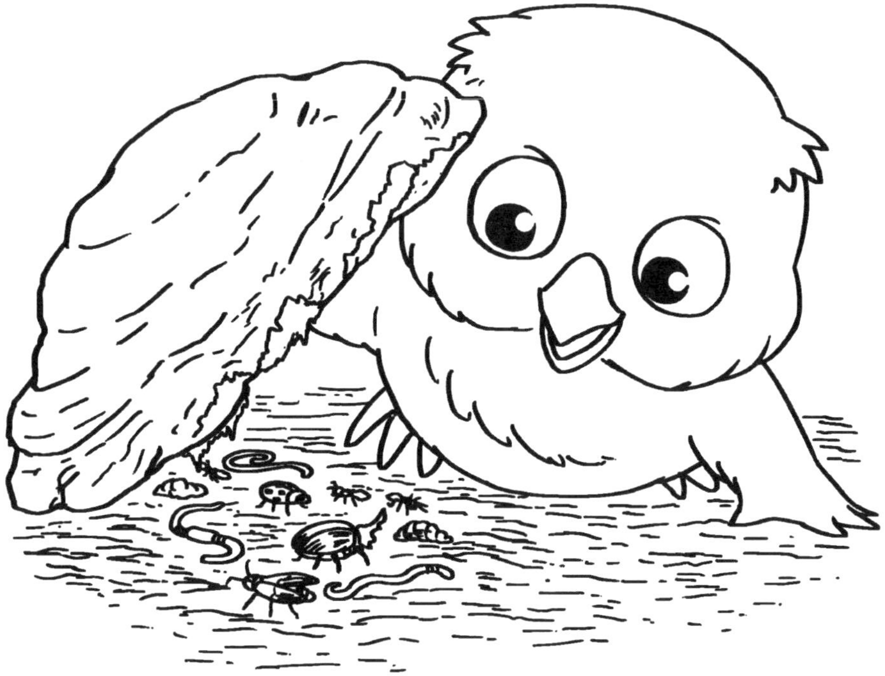

Acknowledgements

Thank you to God, the author and perfecter of my faith.

Thank you to my husband, my encourager and sounding board.

Thank you to my precious sons for being my test subjects and teaching me so much about God's love.

Thank you to my parents for helping to make my dream of writing this book come true.

Thank you to Heather Spronk and Selikke Duthler, from whom I learned much about ministry to young children.

Thank you to the parents, staff, and elders at Bethel Community Church for providing constructive criticism, encouragement, and permission to publish.

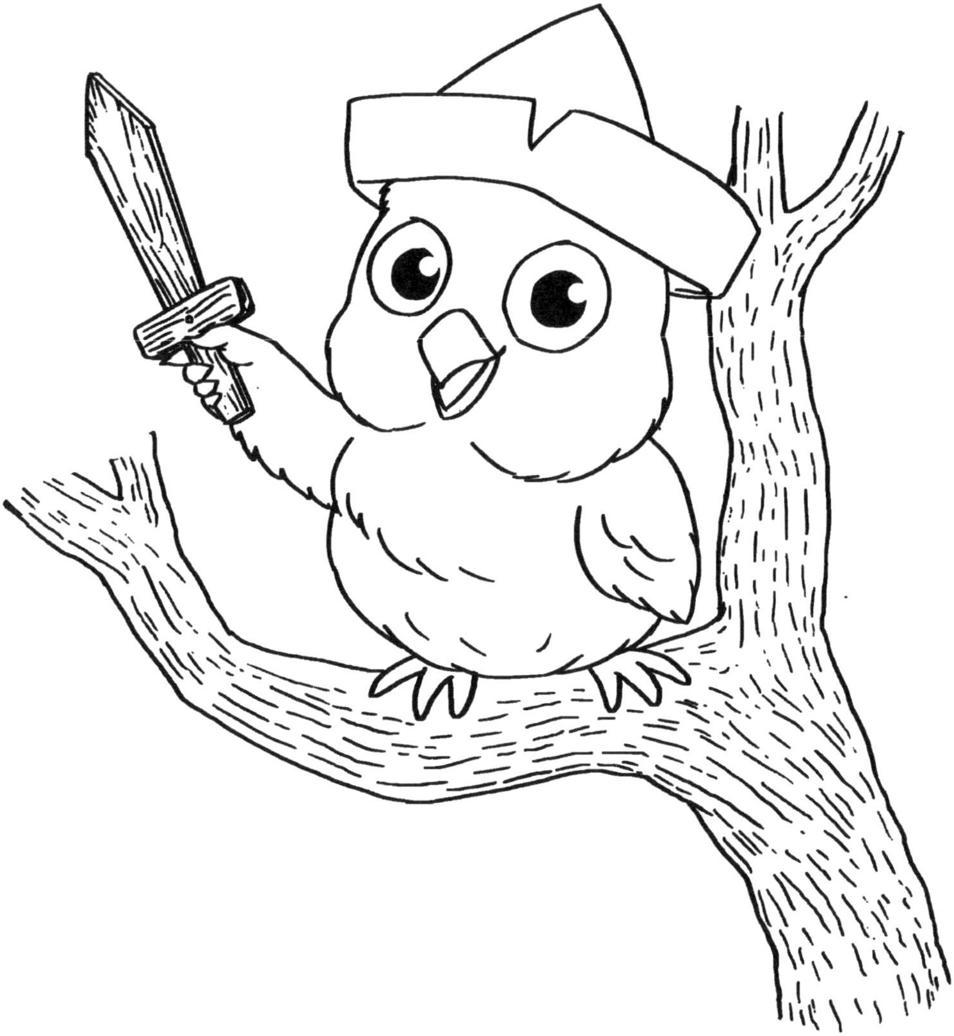

introduction

For over twenty years, I have been working with children in the church, and I have been on staff at a church working in children's ministry since 2004. Most of those years have been spent focused on early childhood, since the early years are my passion and teaching our youngest children is my strength.

Several years ago, I embarked on a quest to find good preschool devotional material to recommend to the parents in my church, and was surprised to discover that most of the books available were either focused on teaching children a set of morals or too abstract for the preschoolers I knew.

Three years ago, I felt a prompting from God to start producing my own devotions for our church families. This book is the compilation of that two-year process. For each of the eighty-five basic Bible stories, I have written a synopsis of the story, five interactive devotions, and a sample prayer.

I had four main objectives when creating the devotions:

1. I believe that parents should be able to follow along with what their children are learning in Sunday school. Therefore, while each devotion is unique, kids interact with the same scripture passage for the entire week. This technique is very beneficial for younger children, as they'll have a chance to truly encounter each story. In some cases, they are able to go deeper into a given story because they'll get more time than the traditional one hour on Sunday.

2. I wanted children to learn according to their own unique learning styles. In general, young children learn through participatory movement and imaginative interaction. To that end, I have incorporated a large array of learning styles into

my devotions. You will find the little owl (Soffy the Owl) indicating the type of activity contained in each devotion. Children will experience God's Word through art, dance, music, Bible memory, Bible reading, and object lessons.

3. I wanted them to be simple. About seventy-five percent of these devotions require no supplies, and those that do only involve accessible items like crayons and paper or stuffed animals. None of the devotions require preparation by the parent. They can be done at bedtime, after supper, in a small group setting, or one-on-one with the child.

4. I wanted preschoolers to learn straight from the Bible. A key focus is the use of actual scripture. While there is a child-friendly paraphrase included in each lesson, most weeks also include having a parent read a small set of verses from the Bible. Usually while this is happening, I have included a small art activity to help children focus. I recommend buying a blank scribbler that your child can draw in each week. When the scribbler is full, you will have a beautiful keepsake of your child's spiritual adventure!

As I wrote these devotions, I had my own boys in mind. They have been my test subjects over the past three years as my husband and I spent time doing the activities with them. It's been such a joy to watch them grow in the knowledge of God and his word, having a lot of fun in the process. My eldest (currently six) really enjoys acting out each story, and usually insists on being the main character. My middle son (currently three) often gives surprising answers to the questions. It's become a family joke that when asked who he would choose to save if he was going to flood the earth, he immediately and unequivocally stated, "Opa." No one else, just Opa!

Wise for Salvation

Even my extended family has had a chance to experience some of the devotions. On a visit to see my husband's parents, we all went marching around the kitchen island, tooting our trumpets and waiting for the walls of Jericho to collapse. It has become a fond family memory that gets dusted off quite often.

In 2 Timothy, Paul admonishes his disciple to...

> Continue in what you have learned and have become convinced of, because you know those from whom you learned it, and how from infancy you have known the holy Scriptures, which are able to make you wise for salvation through faith in Christ Jesus. (2 Timothy 3:14-15, NIV)

Timothy's faith was learned from his grandmother, Lois, and his mother, Eunice. From his earliest days, Timothy was steeped in the knowledge of God, and because of this, he became wise for salvation in Christ Jesus. Not only that, he became a leader in the church at a very young age.

This is what I want for my boys. This is what I want for the children in my church, and for young children all over the world. I want them to be wise for salvation because from infancy they have known the Holy Scriptures. And I hope that this little book will help our children to become wise for salvation at an early age, and become strong Christian leaders as a result.

And while that is happening, I hope you enjoy experiencing the joy and wonder of God's word through little eyes!

Old Testament

When I was in high school, a friend tried to convince me that the Old Testament isn't needed in the Christian faith, that the New Testament is all that's required. I disagreed with him at the time, and as I've grown in my faith I have realized more fully why God gave us the history of Israel.

The New Testament cannot be fully understood without the context of the Old Testament, because Jesus came as a fulfillment of many promises. God promised Abraham that all the peoples of the earth would be blessed through his family. He also promised David that a descendant would always sit on the throne. The prophets spoke of God's promises to save humankind through an incredible sacrifice, and God's people waited for hundreds of years for these promises to be fulfilled.

All of Israel's history culminates in the sacrifice of Jesus on the cross, which is the central tenet of the Christian faith. Even this cannot be fully understood without background knowledge of the first Passover and the sacrificial system of the Old Testament. The context for an innocent atoning for the sin of the guilty was set up thousands of years earlier when Abraham sacrificed a ram in place of his son, and with the implementation of the tabernacle and God's covenant with his people.

There are so many other connections between the Old Testament and the New—associations between events, people, ideas, sacrifices, and celebrations—that I doubt many people truly understand them all.

I don't expect my preschool children to understand the connection between the first Passover and the Last Supper, between the Feast of Firstfruits and Pentecost, or between Joshua and Jesus. However, I do believe that we must give our children a firm foundational understanding of the Old Testament, so that as they grow older they can be amazed by the goodness and faithfulness of God throughout history.

Enjoy these fascinating stories with your child, steeping in them until they become part of the fabric of your family's faith. Through them, see the incredible love of God as he slowly weaves his plan for salvation.

God Makes Light and Dark
Genesis 1:1–5

In the very beginning, everything was dark all the time. There was no sun or moon, no lightbulbs, not even any flashlights. It was just dark. God decided he wanted to create something, so he did. He didn't need any craft supplies or instructions, he only needed his words. So God said, "Let there be light!"—and suddenly there was light! God decided to call it "daytime" when the light was out and "nighttime" when it was dark. And then he said, "It is good!" This was the very first day.

Day 1. Act out the story with your child in a windowless room. Use the light switch to show the difference between day and night.

Day 2. Have your child close her eyes. Together, imagine what it would be like if it was dark all the time. While your child's eyes are closed, read Genesis 1:1–5 straight from the Bible. Have your child open her eyes when it says "And there was light!"

Day 3. *SAY: I wonder why God made the light first. If you got to help God create the whole world, what's the first thing you would create?*

Christie Thomas

Day 4. *ASK: Why do you think God created both day AND night? Why not just daytime? Talk about the kinds of things you do during the day, and the kinds of things you do during the night.*

Day 5. *SAY: Did you know that we can't see colours in the dark? Colours are made from light, so the only time we can see them is when there is light shining! What colours are your favourites?*

PRAYER:

Thank you, God, for creating day and night! I'm so glad that you gave us light and colour, as well as darkness for resting.

Amen.

God Makes Sky and Water
Genesis 1:6–8

The Bible says that in the very beginning, instead of a world, there was just water. On the second day, God decided that he wanted to change that, so he made a sky to go in between the water. He put some water above the sky, in the clouds. That water would fall out of the sky as fat raindrops, sparkly white snowflakes, and chunks of ice. Down below, the whole world was covered with oceans. And then he said, "It is good!"

Day 1. Allow your child to play with some water in a sink as you read him the story (either the paraphrase or from Genesis 1:6–8).

Day 2. *ASK: What kinds of things do we do with water? (Swim, drink, get clean.) What is your favourite thing to do with water? Let's thank God for all the wonderful things we can do with water!*

Day 3. *ASK: Where do we see water in the sky? (Rain, snow.) Why do we have rain? What does it do for the world? (Water the plants.)*

Day 4. *SAY: Let's pretend that we're in an ocean. Let's put on our scuba gear and go swimming!* (Pretend to swim around.) *ASK: What do you see?* (Point out the various living things you might see in the ocean.)

Day 5. *ASK: When our water comes out of the tap, what colour is it? Is it clean or dirty? Did you know that there are lots of kids in the world who have no clean water to drink? They might have to drink out of mud puddles, or places where animals have pooped, or even water that has garbage in it. Do you think that kind of water is healthy for children? No way! Let's pray that these children can get some clean water to drink.*

PRAYER:

Thank you, God, for the gift of water. Thank you for all the important things that water does for us. Help us not to take it for granted or to waste what you've given us, but to always be thankful.

Amen.

God Makes Land, Plants, and Sea
Genesis 1:9–13

On the third day, God separated the water by adding some land in between the different oceans. In the middle of the land were seas, lakes, and rivers. God put all kinds of plants on the land and in the water. From the slimiest seaweed on the bottom of the ocean to the tallest tree on the highest mountain, God made it all! And then he said, "It is good!"

Day 1. Together with your child, pretend to be a plant. Start crouched down like a tiny seed, then slowly grow up into a big plant! *ASK: What kind of plant are you? I'm a _____! Did God make you? He sure did!*

Day 2. *ASK: Did you know that plants make air for us to breathe? I guess they're pretty important! What else do we do with plants? (Flowers for decoration, fruits/veggies to eat, big trees for shade…)*

Day 3. *SAY: When God made land, he made all kinds of land. There are mountains, valleys, flat grassy lands, deserts, hills, forests, even lands full of snow and ice! What kind of land would you like to visit?*

Day 4. *ASK: How many kinds of plants did God make? Lots and lots! Let's see if we can think of some—tomato plants, apple trees, flowers, grass, Christmas trees, seaweed, moss… (Insert your favourite plant here.) Why do you think God made so many different kinds?*

Day 5. *ASK: Do you know what kinds of things plants need to grow? (Light, water, dirt.) Who made all those things? God did! He made the light on the first day, the water on the second day, and the dirt on the third day. Wow, God sure thought of everything! Isn't he smart?*

PRAYER:

Thank you, God, for making all the biggest things in our world-the mountains, the giant oceans, and the tallest tree. Thank you for making the smallest things too-the tiniest plant in the ocean and the smallest piece of dirt.

Amen.

God Makes the Sun, Moon, and Stars
Genesis 1:14–19

Even though God had made day and night, he hadn't put anything in the sky to make light. So on the fourth day, God made the bright yellow sun to give light during the day, and the glowing moon and stars to give light at night. And then he said, "It is good!"

Day 1. Read the paraphrase or actual text of Genesis 1:14–19 to your child, then sing "Twinkle, Twinkle" together.

Day 2. While cupping your hands into a pretend telescope, look up at the sky. *ASK: Do you know how many stars are in the sky? I don't! Let's guess, though. Maybe three hundred million billion and ten! Why do you think God made so many stars?*

Day 3. *ASK: Where does the sun go at night? Where does the moon go during the day? Why do you think God wanted us to have a sun and a moon?*

Day 4. *SAY: Let's learn something about God's amazing creation— the moon!* One of you should stand still and pretend to be the earth, while the other walks in a slow circle around the "earth." *SAY: Our moon goes all the way around the earth, once a day, every day.*

Day 5. Read Psalm 113:3 with your child. *SAY: This verse tells us that we should praise God all day. Let's praise God right now! Either pray your praises or sing a favourite praise song together.*

PRAYER:

Thank you, God, for putting the sun, moon, and stars in the sky so we can see. You are so great and powerful. How amazing you are!

Amen.

God Makes Fish and Birds

Genesis 1:19–23

After God made the oceans and the land and the sky, he decided to fill the world up with animals! On day five, He made birds to swoop and glide in the sky, and fish to swish around in the water. From enormous whales and toothy sharks to hummingbirds and magpies, God made them all. And then he said, "It is good!"

Day 1. Read Genesis 1:19–23 and act out every kind of creature that you read about (you'll be alternating underwater creatures and birds several times).

Day 2. Make some bird sounds together with your child. What kind of birds do you hear in your neighbourhood? On a farm? In the forest? At a lake?[1]

Day 3. *ASK: What kinds of animals can you think of that live in the water? I wonder why God made so many kinds. Why do you think God made sharks?*

---

1 *If you have internet access, go to* <u>enature.com/birding/audio.asp</u> *and listen to some bird calls.*

Day 4. *ASK: Have you ever seen a flamingo? How about a penguin? I wonder if God made some birds just to make him laugh. What fish or birds do you think are pretty crazy looking?*

Day 5. Practice saying Genesis 1:31 together: "God saw all that he had made, and it was very good" (NIV). Try saying it while making a bubbling sound with your finger on your lips (as a fish) and while flapping your arms (as a bird).

PRAYER:

Thank you, God, for making so many interesting animals to live in the air and water. You are the wonderful God who creates everything for your joy—and our joy too! Help us see how amazing your creation is this week.

Amen.

God Makes Land Animals
Genesis 1:24–25

On day six, God decided to make some more animals; this time he wanted animals on land. God made every kind of animal you could ever dream of—goofy monkeys, giant dinosaurs, tiny bugs, slow sloths, and speedy cheetahs. And then he said, "It is good!"

Day 1. Read Genesis 1:24–25 and act out every kind of creature you read about.

Day 2. *SAY: The Bible says that Adam, the first man, got to name all the animals. Let's collect some stuffed animals and give them all names! What kind of sounds do these animals make?*

Day 3. *ASK: If you could ride on any animal in the whole world, which animal would you choose? If you could have any animal as a pet, which animal would you choose?*

Day 4. Play animal charades with your child. One person pretends to be an animal and the other has to guess what it is! (Some ideas: crocodiles, butterflies, snakes, lions, monkeys, mosquitoes…)

Day 5. *SAY: In the Bible (Genesis 1:28) it says that people are supposed to rule over animals. That means that we are in charge of them, but we also need to take care of them. Can you think of a way that our family takes care of animals?* (Maybe you have a pet, help worms get back into the ground after it rains, put out a bird feeder, or wait for ducks to cross the road.)

PRAYER:

God, you are so creative and we thank you for making such an amazing amount of animals for us to enjoy. Help us to look after the animals of the world just like Adam and Eve did.

Amen.

God Makes People
Genesis 1:26–27

God had made all kinds of creatures in all sizes and shapes. But he still wanted to make someone in his image—someone he could talk to. God reached down into the dust and created Adam out of it. When he was done with Adam, he created Eve out of Adam's rib. He gave them hearts for loving, souls for worshipping, minds for thinking, and bodies for living. When he was done making people, God said, "It is *very* good!" They were his very favourite creation and he loved them very much.

Day 1. Use your bodies to have some fun with your child—do the hokey-pokey or sing "Head and Shoulders" together!

Day 2. Draw an outline of a person (or a stick figure). Together with your child, fill in features that belong to them, like the colour of eyes and hair, or what they're wearing.

Day 3. Look in a mirror. *SAY: Did you know that you are God's most special creation? Which part of your body is your favourite?*

Christie Thomas

Day 4. *ASK: How many fingers do you have? How many toes? How many eyes, ears, and noses? How many belly buttons? God made your body so special!*

Day 5. Have your child draw a picture of a person while you read Genesis 1:26–27. *ASK: What do you think it means that God made us in his image? Why do you think God likes people the best of all his creations?*

PRAYER:

Dear God, thank you for making us all special. Thank you especially for making my child, and for making him/her perfect for our family.

Amen.

God Makes the Garden
Genesis 2:8–15

God loved the people he had made very much, so he wanted care of them. He made a beautiful garden for them to live in. In the garden there were rivers to drink from, trees to climb and eat fruit from, leaves to protect them from the hot sun, and a soft ground to sleep on at night.

Day 1. Cup your hands together and imagine that you are holding an egg. Talk about how chickens lay them so we can have food. *ASK: What other kinds of food do we eat? Where does it come from? What is your favourite thing to eat?*

Day 2. *SAY: God gave Adam and Eve a home, and he gives us a home too.* Walk through your home and thank God for each part of it—the roof, the floor, the walls, the windows, the beds, etc. Pray for children who don't have a home.

Day 3. We know that God provides for us, and he also uses us to help provide for other people. Go through some of your things and choose a few (food, toys, etc.) to give to someone in need.

Day 4. Turn on the water tap. *ASK: Did you know that in lots of countries, children have to collect water in a bucket from a well or lake before they can drink or take a bath?* Thank God for indoor plumbing, and pray for children who need clean water.

Day 5. Have your child draw a picture of a garden while you read Genesis 2:8–15. Review all the things that God has given to you. *ASK: Why do you think God wants to take care of us?*

PRAYER:

Dear God, thank you for all that you've provided for our family. Thank you specifically for _____.

  Amen.

God Takes a Rest

Genesis 2:1–3

God made the world and everything in it. That must have been a lot of work! So after working hard for six days, God took a day off. The Bible says that he "rested." God gives us times of rest too, and created us to need it.

Day 1. Lay down with your child. *SAY: God took a rest after creating everything, and he made us with the need to rest as well. That's why we sleep!* (It might help a sleep-fighting preschooler to know that even God took a rest!) *Why do you think God made our bodies to need sleep? What do you think might happen if we never went to sleep?*

Day 2. Clean up your child's room together. Afterward, take a rest. *ASK: Why do you think God decided he needed a rest?*

Day 3. *ASK: What helps you relax? What makes you feel happy and peaceful?*

Day 4. Read Genesis 2:1–3. *ASK: If you were God, what would you do on your day of rest? (Maybe he naps with a blanket made of stars, or swings from a rainbow, or sits on his throne and watches his favourite animals!)*

Day 5. Usually when we sleep, we dream. *ASK: Can you remember any of your dreams? Sometimes we have bad dreams that scare us. Let's ask God to help us rest in peace tonight.*

PRAYER:

Thank you, God, for all the wonderful things you created. I pray that everyone would know and understand that you created them special and that you created all these things for us. Help us to rest peacefully in your love tonight.

Amen.

Noah Builds an Ark
Genesis 6–7:16

God had a plan to wash all the badness from the earth, but he wanted to save someone very special. That special person was named Noah. Noah loved God, so God told him that in order to be saved from the big washing, he would have to build a boat. But this would not be a motorboat or a sailboat! This boat was to be made out of wood, and big enough to hold two of every kind of animal on the earth! Noah didn't even see any water around him, but he obeyed God because he knew that God keeps his promises. God sent a big storm to wash away everything on the earth, but Noah, his family, and the animals were safe on the ark.

Day 1. *SAY: The Bible says that God told Noah how to build the ark. Let's use our imaginations and see if we can think of how God might have done that. Do you think God's voice boomed from heaven? Do you think he came and stood in front of Noah? Did God talk to him while Noah was dreaming? How do you think God talked to Noah? Let's be like Noah and obey God by building an ark.* (Pretend to use a hammer and saw to build a big boat!)

Day 2. *ASK: Do you know why God wanted Noah to build a boat for saving his family and the animals? What was God going to do to the earth? Why do you think he wanted to do that?* Remind your child that while God wanted to get rid of all the badness on the earth once, he promised he would never wash the whole earth again.

Day 3. *ASK: Yesterday we talked about how God wanted to wash the earth clean and start over. Why do you think he saved Noah?* (See Genesis 7:1 for the answer.) *If you were going to wash the earth clean, who would you want to save?*

Day 4. *SAY: One of the things that God did was send two of every kind of animal to the ark. Let's pretend to be some of those animals now! We need a boy lion/monkey/snake/mosquito and a girl lion/monkey/snake/mosquito. Let's go to the ark...*

Day 5. Sit on a bed or couch together and pretend that you are on the ark in the middle of forty days of storms. Rock back and forth, take care of the animals, and act a little seasick. *ASK: What do you think Noah and his family thought about when they were in the longest storm ever? Will God keep his promise to keep Noah safe?*

PRAYER:

Thank you, God, for your promise to love and protect us. Thank you for keeping your promises to Noah. Thank you for bringing the animals to the ark and protecting them during the flood. Help us to trust and obey you like Noah did.

Amen.

The Great Flood
Genesis 8:1–22; 9:8–17

After Noah, his family, and the animals climbed into the ark, God closed the door of the giant boat. Then he made it rain… and rain… and rain for forty days and forty nights. That's a long time! Noah and his family and the animals waited in the ark for almost a year. That's like waiting from one birthday all the way to the next birthday. What a long time to live on a boat! Finally, the ground was dry again. After they got off the ark, God promised Noah that he would never flood the earth again. He put a rainbow in the sky as a reminder of his promise.

Day 1. Make a big noisy storm! Slap your knees to make rain, crash and boom to make thunder, and flicker the lights to make lightening. *ASK: Do you think Noah's family was scared? Would you have been scared? Why?*

Day 2. Help your child draw a picture of something that makes them afraid. *ASK: Did you know that God is always with you, just like he was with Noah on the ark?*

Day 3. Read Noah's story from a children's Bible. *ASK: What is your favourite part of the story? Why?*

Day 4. Look at the back of a CD or DVD to see if you can find the rainbow reflection. *ASK: Do you see the rainbow? Why did God put a rainbow in the sky? Have you ever seen a rainbow outside?*

Day 5. Look around the room and find things that match each colour of the rainbow. Thank God for putting the rainbow in the sky to remind us that he keeps his promises.

PRAYER:

Thank you, God, for protecting Noah in the ark, and for giving us your promises. We know that you always keep your promises.

Amen.

Joseph the Dreamer
Genesis 37, 39–40

Joseph had a lot of brothers, and they didn't like him very much. God gave him dreams at night that showed that one day he would be in charge of them. They got jealous of him and wanted to hurt him. One day, while they were out in the fields, they stole Joseph's clothes, beat him up, and threw him in a big hole! But God was with Joseph in the hole. Then his brothers sold Joseph to some men who would use Joseph as a slave! But even when he became a slave in Egypt, God was with Joseph. He had many adventures as a slave, and even had to spend some time in jail, but even there God was with Joseph.

Day 1. After reading the story to your kids, act it out together.

Day 2. *SAY: Joseph's brothers did these horrible things because they were jealous of and mad at Joseph. Have you ever gotten really mad at someone? Maybe a brother or a sister or a friend? What did you do? What do you think God wants us to do when we get angry? (The first thing I would encourage is to talk to God about it! He will help us do the right thing.)*

Day 3. Read the story directly from the Bible (Genesis 37:23–36) while your child draws a picture of Joseph's fancy coat. If your child has questions about all the bad things that happened to Joseph, remind them that God was with Joseph, even in this, and that God had a plan for Joseph's life.

Day 4. Use this little experiment to teach your child what jealousy is. You will need an item that your child likes—perhaps a candy, a favourite blankie, or anything else that will entice your child.

If you are doing this with only one child, show the child the item. Then very deliberately keep it for yourself. Really ham it up so that your child experiences the emotions. *SAY: This is mine. Oh I love it so much. I'm so glad I have it.* If you are doing this with more than one child, give the item to the youngest child, and just sit back and watch the jealously emerge! *SAY: Tell me how you're feeling right now. I think you're feeling jealous. It's not a nice feeling, is it? That's how Joseph's brothers felt. They were jealous that their daddy gave Joseph some fancy new clothes and didn't give any to them. When we feel jealous, we need to talk to God about our feelings, and let him help us do the right thing.*

Wise for Salvation

Day 5. *ASK: How do you think Joseph felt when he was all alone in that pit? How about when he was sold to be a slave? How about when he got sent to jail even though he didn't do anything wrong? One thing that Joseph knew was that God had plans for him. He knew that God was with him always.* Practice memorizing a verse together: *"I am with you always…"* (Matthew 28:20, NIV).

PRAYER:

Thank you, God, that you were in all those sad and lonely places with Joseph. Thank you for leading him and showing him that you were working out his life for the good. Help us to trust that you are always with us as well, even when life is hard.

Amen.

Joseph the Forgiver

Genesis 41–45

While Joseph was in jail, Pharaoh had a very strange dream. He found out that Joseph could interpret dreams, so Pharaoh had Joseph brought to him. God showed Joseph the meaning of Pharaoh's dream, and Pharaoh was so happy that he put Joseph in charge of the whole country! After a few years, there was a great famine in the land, which meant that no food could grow. People became very hungry. But because God helped Joseph plan for the famine, there was food in Egypt. Even Joseph's brothers finally had to come to Egypt to ask for some food. When they got there, it was a big surprise to everyone that Joseph was in charge of Egypt! Joseph told them who he was, and then he forgave them for selling him as a slave. Forgiveness is something that is *very* hard to do, but God helped Joseph to do it.

Day 1. After reading the story to your kids, act it out together.

Day 2. *SAY: God was with Joseph when he was in charge of the country. God helped him to do this very hard thing. Have you ever had to do something that was hard for you?* (Go to a day camp alone, do a chore that was difficult, or be kind to a sibling.) *Did you know that God promises to always be with you, no matter what hard things you have to do? Let's ask God to help us remember that!* (Pray.)

Wise for Salvation

Day 3. Read the story of Joseph from a children's Bible while your child draws a picture of Joseph and his brothers.

Day 4. *SAY: Joseph's brothers had to travel all the way from their country to Egypt just to get some food. How do you think they felt when they got there? How do you feel when you're really hungry? Let's pretend that we're really hungry.* (Rub your tummy and groan.) *I'm so glad that God had a plan for how he was going to feed Joseph's brothers. He used their terrible plan to hurt Joseph to get Joseph into Egypt, and to get him in charge of the country, and to save food so that Joseph's brothers could come buy some and be saved! Sometimes God does some pretty strange and amazing things!*

Day 5. You will need a piece of paper, a crayon/marker, and a Band-Aid. Draw a heart on the paper. *SAY: Sometimes people hurt us, just like Joseph's brothers hurt him. Can you think of a time when someone hurt you?* When your child has an answer, write it down in the heart, then draw a jagged line through the heart to make it look broken. *SAY: When people hurt us, it can feel like our heart is broken. Sometimes they do it on purpose and sometimes they don't even know that our heart is hurt. But God wants us to forgive them. The only way to really heal this broken heart is for us to forgive that person. Forgiving someone*

29

means that we stop being mad at them. Can you stop being mad at the person who hurt you? Let's put a Band-Aid on that heart to show our forgiveness. Sometimes forgiveness is really hard, but we can ask God to help us.

PRAYER:

Help us, God, to forgive like Joseph did. We know it wasn't easy for him to forgive his brothers, but thank you for helping him to do it. May we always remember to ask you for help when we're having trouble stopping being mad at someone.

Amen.

Baby Moses
Exodus 1:22–2:10

There was a terrible king in Egypt, called Pharaoh, and he hated God's people, the Israelites. He made a law that every Israelite baby boy was supposed to be thrown into the river! But one mommy got really brave and smart, and she put her son in a basket in the river. Soon a princess came by and she found the baby! She decided to adopt him, so this baby ended up living in the palace with Pharaoh. This baby's name was Moses. God had great plans for Moses later in his life, so he protected him while he was a baby.

Day 1. Act out the story with your child using a stuffed toy or a doll as Moses. (Or your child can pretend to be baby Moses if they like to be silly!)

Day 2. *SAY: God protected baby Moses. Is there anyone in your life who could use God's protection right now? Maybe you have a friend who's sick, or maybe you're just learning how to ride a bike and you keep hurting yourself. Maybe your mom is going to have a baby or your grandpa is going on a long trip. Who should we pray for today?*

Day 3. Take care of a baby doll together (or stuffed animal). *ASK: How do parents take care of their babies? Let's do some of those things for this baby. Moses' mommy wanted him to be safe, so she took care of him in a very unusual way!*

Day 4. Read the story right from the Bible (Exodus 1:22–2:10) or from a children's Bible while your child draws a picture of a basket.

Day 5. *SAY: God uses other people to take care of us, just like he used Miriam and the princess to take care of Moses. Who takes care of you? How do they take care of you?*

PRAYER:

God, thank you for protecting baby Moses. Please protect me, because I know you have big plans for me too!

Amen.

Burning Bush
Exodus 3:1–10, 4:1–17

When Moses grew up, he left Egypt and became a shepherd in the desert. One day, he saw something strange—a bush that was on fire but didn't burn up! Then the bush got even more weird—it started to talk! It was God talking to him. Moses was very scared, but God told him that he had chosen Moses to go set the Israelites free from Pharaoh and the Egyptians. Moses' special job was to go ask Pharaoh to let all his people go free. Moses was even more scared when he heard this! But God gave him courage, and Moses obeyed.

Day 1. Act out the story with your child or read the paraphrase. Go ahead and ham it up!

Day 2. *SAY: Even though Moses knew that God is great and very powerful, he was still scared to talk to the mean Pharaoh. Are there any things that God could help you not be scared about? Maybe you're kind of scared of preschool or your babysitter, or maybe you're scared of the dark. Let's talk to God about that right now.*

Day 3. Read the story right from the Bible (Exodus 3:1–10, 4:1–17) or from a children's Bible while your child draws a picture of a fire.

Day 4. *SAY: God asked Moses to take off his sandals because he was standing on holy ground, which meant that he was standing close to God. It also says that Moses covered his face because he was afraid to look at God. We don't have to be afraid to talk to God, but let's take off our socks now and pray that God will stand close to us! We can cover our faces too and pretend to be like Moses.*

Day 5. *SAY: God told Moses what to do, and he (eventually) did it. Let's practice our obeying right now with a fun little game.* Play Simon Says with your child. *ASK: What did we learn from this? Do you think it was easy for Moses to do what God asked? Why did he do it anyway?*

PRAYER:

God, thank you for seeing the needs of your people and sending someone to help them. Help me to listen and obey too when you give me a job.

Amen.

Plagues
Exodus 7:14–10:29

Moses went to talk to Pharaoh about letting the Israelites go free, but Pharaoh was really mean and said "No!" God showed his amazing power to Pharaoh by making lots of crazy things happen to the Egyptians, things called "plagues." He made millions of frogs and bugs come into their houses, and even to be in their food! Then he made everyone get really sick and all kinds of other bad things happened. God did this because he wanted Pharaoh to find out how great and powerful God is. But after each plague was gone, Moses would ask Pharaoh to let the people go, and each time Pharaoh said "No!" Finally, plague number ten made Pharaoh really sad and he told Moses to take the Israelites and leave. Pharaoh had definitely learned that God is great and very powerful. The best part was that the Israelites didn't have to be slaves anymore!

Day 1. Act out the story with your child or read the paraphrase. Use as many plagues in your in your re-enactment as you like. A few are inappropriate for preschoolers, but here is a list: water turns to blood, frogs, gnats/lice, flies, sick animals, sores on the skin, hail, locusts, darkness, and the death of the firstborn.

Day 2. *SAY: God made all those bad things happen to Pharaoh and his people, but it was important for teaching them about his power. Are there any bad things that are happening in your life right now?* Maybe somebody is sick or you have to move, or your family gets mad at each other a lot. Think of something, then pray together.

Day 3. Read the story from a children's Bible (if it has this story) while your child draws a picture of a frog or a bug. The full biblical story is way too long for a preschooler's attention span, but you can skim Exodus 7–10 and give your child the highlights while he or she colours.

Day 4. One of the plagues was that there were bugs *everywhere*. Pretend to be like bugs and hop/fly around. *ASK: How do you think the people of Egypt liked this plague? Pretty gross, isn't it? Why do you think Pharaoh kept changing his mind over and over again, even when God kept sending terrible plagues on his people?*

Day 5. Memorize the following Bible verse together while pretending to be a frog: *"Our Lord is great and very powerful"* (Psalm 147:5, NCV).

PRAYER:

God, you are great and very powerful. Thank you for showing Pharaoh, the Israelites, and Moses how amazing and powerful you are.

Amen.

Escape through the Sea
Exodus 14:1–29

God's people left Egypt and started walking to the Promised Land. God led his people to the edge of the Red Sea, but suddenly Pharaoh decided he didn't want to let them go after all. He gathered all his soldiers with their swords, horses, and chariots—and they started chasing God's people to try to get them back. The Israelites were very, very afraid, but God protected them. He sent a big wind to do something amazing—it blew the sea wide open so the people could walk across the Red Sea on a dry path! Then, when Pharaoh's army tried to chase the Israelites, God made the water crash back down so they couldn't catch God's people anymore. They were finally free!

Day 1. Act out the story with your child and/or read the paraphrase.

Day 2. *SAY: Moses and his people were really, really scared, but God helped them to be brave. Do you know anyone who is brave? Let's see if we can think of some brave people around us. Or maybe even a time when you have been brave.* (Talk about Daddy driving carefully in a storm or Mommy starting a new job. Perhaps your child is taking swimming lessons and being brave even when they go underwater.) Pray about whatever comes up in the conversation.

Day 3. *SAY: Yesterday we said that Moses and his people were brave to walk right through the Red Sea. Do you know why Moses was brave? Because he knew that God was with him and God could protect him. Do you know why you can be brave? Because God is with you too! And he can protect you.*

Day 4. Read the story right from the Bible (Exodus 14:1–29) or from a children's Bible while your child draws a picture of the sea.

Day 5. Get a bowl of water or fill up a sink with water. Ask your child to blow really hard and try to make a path in the middle of the water. *SAY: Can you do it? Who is the only one who can do such an amazing miracle? Why did he do that miracle?*

PRAYER:

Thank you, God, for protecting the Israelites and saving them from their enemies! Please protect me and help me to be brave.

Amen.

God Leads His People
Exodus 13:21–22

When God's people left Egypt, they didn't know where to go. Some people thought they should go this way, and someone else thought they should go that way. Thankfully, God guided them by setting a big pillar of cloud before them in the daytime, and changing it into a pillar of fire in the night. That way, the Israelites always knew that God was with them, and that he would guide them. All they had to do was follow the pillar of cloud and fire!

Day 1. Act out the story with your child and/or read the paraphrase.

Day 2. *SAY: God's people got to see that God was with them always, because they could always see the pillar of cloud or fire. We can't see God like that, but he is still with us! Let's write down some places where God is with us. Is God with us at home? Church? The grocery store? At swimming lessons? Preschool? Let's thank God for being with us in those places!*

Day 3. Read the story right from the Bible (Exodus 13:21–22) or from a children's Bible while your child draws a picture of a cloud or fire.

Day 4. Look at a map together (on a computer, phone, or an actual paper map). *SAY: God's people didn't have a map to follow to the Promised Land. Instead they had to just trust that God would take them the right way. We don't have a pillar of cloud or fire to follow, but what are some ways we can learn to follow God in our lives?*

Day 5. Play "Follow the Leader" and remind your child that the Israelites had to follow the pillars of cloud and fire, because that was God's way of showing them where to go!

PRAYER:

Thank you, God, for your promise to be with us and guide us. Help us to follow you always!

Amen.

God Provides

Exodus 16:4–18, 31; 17:1–7

The Israelites were finally safe from the mean Pharaoh, but now they were stuck in the desert where there was no food or water! They whined and complained to Moses because their tummies were so hungry and their bodies were so thirsty. Moses talked to God about it, and God sent them food in a very strange way. When the people woke up in the morning, there was a strange kind of bread all over the ground. They ate it, and they called it "manna." At night there was meat on the ground for them to gather and eat. God also made water come pouring out of a rock for them to drink.

Day 1. Act out the story with your child, using yourselves as characters. Or you can ham it up with lots of stuffed animals complaining about the living conditions!

Day 2. Pretend to hold a heavy rock (or if you have one around, hold a real one). Try to drink from it. *SAY: Mmmm, what tasty water this is. What? This isn't a glass of water? Well, what is it? A rock? Oh dear, but I'm really thirsty! Hey, do you remember that story from the Bible about how God made water come from a rock? Do you think I could do that? Nope, only God can. Why did he do that?* (They were in the desert, there was no water to drink, he cared for them.) *Does God care for you too?*

Day 3. Take a field trip to the kitchen to check out the contents of your fridge/cupboards/freezer. Talk about what kinds of food you have and the kinds of food God gave to the Israelites in the desert. Isn't our God so great and powerful?

Day 4. Read the story right from the Bible (Exodus 16:4–18, 31, and 17:1–6) or from a children's Bible while your child draws a picture of their favourite food.

Day 5. *ASK: What is your favourite part of this Bible story? What type of food do you think you would have liked the best? (Crackers or meat.) What would you think if there were crackers all over the grass outside when you woke up tomorrow morning?*

PRAYER:

God, thank you for giving the Israelites something to eat and drink even though they were cranky grumblers. Help us to remember that we can trust you with all of our needs because you are great and very powerful!

Amen.

God's Rules
Exodus 19:16–20:21

In the desert, God told Moses that he would visit the people in a cloud. But this wasn't just any cloud: it was a huge, ginormous cloud that covered a whole mountain! The cloud was filled with lightning and thunder and coming from it was a loud trumpet blast. The mountain was covered in smoke because God came down on the mountain in a fire. The mountain shook, and the sound of trumpets grew louder and louder. The people were terrified with a capital T! In the middle of the noise and smoke, God called to Moses to climb up the mountain. Moses did, and while he was there, God gave him ten rules written on a big piece of stone. When he came down, Moses was in charge of teaching the rules to the people.

This week, we're going to summarize some of the rules. Feel free to share the others with your child if you feel they need to hear one that isn't covered.

Day 1. *SAY: The most important rule to remember is that God is the most important. Why do you think God wants to be the most important? What kinds of things can get in the way of God being number one? How can we make sure God is always number one in our lives?* Pray together, asking God to help you make him number one in your lives.

Day 2. *SAY: Another one of God's rules is that we are supposed to love and obey our mommies and daddies. What are some ways you can do that?* Ask God to help you and your child honour your and their parents.

Day 3. *SAY: Another one of God's rules is that we shouldn't want what others have, or try to take what others have. This is a really hard one, isn't it? Can you think of a time when you wanted something that someone else had? Can you think of a time when you took something that wasn't yours?* Pray together, asking God to help you to be content with what you have and not try to take things that aren't yours.

Note: I'm sure you've noticed this is a struggle for all children! I feel that the biggest way to help children not covet is to teach them thankfulness—when we are grateful and content in our lives, we are much less likely to covet, steal, and commit adultery.

Day 4. *SAY: God also wants us to be truthful. What does that mean? Pray about it together, asking God to help you and your child be truthful.* Note: most small children don't lie; they just tell stories and play make-believe. This rule isn't against using imagination. Lying is about telling something untrue with the purpose of misleading them. If your child is five years old or higher, they mostly likely have lied to you before.

Day 5. *SAY: Another of God's most important rules is that we should love others instead of hurting them. How can we do that today?* Pray about it together!

Wise for Salvation

PRAYER:

Thank you, God, for your rules, and that you give them to us because you love us. Help us to love you and obey you.

Amen.

Spies and Rahab

Joshua 2:1–22, 6:23

God's people were finally ready to get out of the desert and into the Promised Land. The problem was, there were people already living there! So the new leader, Joshua, sent two spies to check out the city of Jericho. There were some bad guys who wanted to catch the spies, so a lady named Rahab hid them under some flax. She knew God, and knew that the Israelites were going to take over the city, so she asked the spies to save her and her family. They promised that if she kept a red rope hanging from her window, they would be able to save her. So they climbed out of the city down the red rope in the middle of the night, and ran back to Joshua. Later, when the walls of Jericho came tumbling down, the spies found Rahab and her family and saved them.

Day 1. Act out the story with your child, using yourselves as characters. (Or just read the paraphrased story with gusto!)

Day 2. Gather something red—a ribbon, a pair of pants, a belt, a shirt—anything long and skinny will do. *SAY: The Bible says that Rahab knew all the things God had done for the Israelites when they were in the desert (like opening up the Red Sea) and that she believed in God because of those things.* Tie your red item somewhere where he/she will see it (the doorknob, a bedframe). *SAY: Just like Rahab, we can know about the things that God has done and believe in God because of those things. Let's let this red item remind us of how God saved Rahab and the spies.*

Wise for Salvation

Day 3. Option 1: Play a short game of hide-and-seek with your child. Option 2: Hide under a blanket together while you discuss the story. *ASK: Do you think the spies were scared when the bad guys came to where they were hiding? Where would you hide from a bad guy? I'm so glad that God protected the spies, and God protects you too!*

Day 4. Read the story right from the Bible (Joshua 2:1–22, 6:23) or from a children's Bible while your child draws a picture of a red rope.

Day 5. Pretend to be spies together. Skulk around your house, sneaking around corners and using silly hand gestures. *ASK: What do you see? Are there any bad guys around? What would you look for if you were looking for a new place to live?*

PRAYER:

God, you are great and very powerful. Thank you for protecting the spies from the bad guys, and for saving Rahab and her family because she loved you.

Amen.

Jericho

Joshua 6:6–20

God's people were ready to take over the city of Jericho. The city was full of people who didn't like God, so God wanted his people to have it instead. They didn't know how to get in because there were *really* big walls made out of rock all around the city, but God gave them a strange plan. They marched around the city once a day for six days. Then, on the seventh day, they walked around the city seven whole times! The last time they walked around, the people made as much noise as they could—they screamed and shouted and blasted their trumpets super loud. The walls started to crack, and then the walls started to crumble, and then the big, thick, sturdy rock walls came crashing down! God's people climbed over the fallen walls and took over the city.

Day 1. Act out the story with your child and/or read the paraphrase.

Day 2. Look out a window with your child and pretend that you see an army of people marching around your house. *SAY: What would you think about that? Would you be scared or maybe think the people were being a little silly?*

Wise for Salvation

Day 3. *ASK: What would you have done to knock down the walls of a city? What do you think of God's plan for taking over Jericho? Sometimes God's plans don't make any sense to us, but when we trust him, we discover that he does some pretty amazing things! Can you think of some other amazing things that God has done?*

Day 4. Read the story right from the Bible (Joshua 6:6–20) or from a children's Bible while your child draws a picture of a pile of rocks.

Day 5. Pretend to toot a horn, then practice memorizing the following verse: *"Our Lord is great and very powerful"* (Psalm 147:5, NCV).

PRAYER:

Thank you, God, for knocking down the walls of Jericho! Help us to trust you to do amazing things in our lives too.

Amen.

Gideon's Army

Judges 7:1–21

At a time when God's people were finally living in the Promised Land, there were some people who really didn't like them. In fact, there was a big bad army that wanted to hurt God's people! God asked a man named Gideon to get an army ready to fight them. Lots of people signed up to fight the bad guys, but God wanted him to have a teeny tiny army instead. He wanted his people to always remember that God had done the saving, not the army. So Gideon sent some of the people home. Then Gideon took his teeny tiny army and gave them each a trumpet and a light inside a jar. They surrounded the big bad army in the middle of the night and gave them a big scare! They blew their trumpets and smashed their jars, and God made the big bad army so afraid that they started fighting with each other instead of with Gideon's army! The rest of them ran away and God's people were saved!

Day 1. Read the paraphrase and/or act out the story with your child.

Day 2. Practice memorizing a verse together: *"Trust in the Lord with all your heart"* (Proverbs 3:5, NIV). Try saying it like a big scary army and like a little teeny tiny army. *ASK: How did Gideon have to trust God? What can you trust God about?*

Wise for Salvation

Day 3. SAY: The people in the big bad army were called Midianites, and they were really mean to God's people. Have you ever met someone who wasn't very kind to you? If so, let's talk to God about that person and ask him to help us trust in him with all our hearts.

Day 4. Either use your imagination to pretend you have a flashlight, or get a real one for this activity. Pretend that you are in Gideon's army. Sneak around your house and get to a dark place (like a bathroom), then blow your pretend trumpets, turn on your lights or the flashlight, and shout "For the Lord and for Gideon!" like his army did.

Day 5. Have your child draw a picture of a trumpet or a light while you read the story straight from the Bible (Judges 7:1–21), or a from a children's Bible.

PRAYER:

Thank you, Lord, for showing Gideon and his army that they could trust you to win the battle, even with a teeny tiny army! You really are great and powerful, God.

Amen.

Ruth and Naomi

Ruth 1

Naomi and her family moved away from the town of Bethlehem because there was no food to eat. They walked very far away and lived in the country of Moab. A long time later, Naomi's husband and two sons got sick and died. The only family she had left were the ladies who had been married to her sons. She was very sad, so she decided to go back home. She packed up her things and started walking. Naomi told the ladies that they should stay in Moab. One of them, the lady named Ruth, decided to stay with Naomi. Ruth left the country she knew, the family she had grown up with, and the friends she loved, and went with Noami to Bethlehem. They didn't know where they would live or what they would eat, but they did have each other. When they got to Bethlehem, Ruth took care of Naomi by picking barley from the fields for them to eat.

Day 1. Read the paraphrase and/or act out the story with your child. Be sure to walk a long, long way through your house!

Day 2. Gather a bunch of similar small items (like scraps of paper or small toys). *SAY: Ruth did something called "gleaning," which is when she picked up the leftover barley from someone else's field. Let's try gleaning! I will put some stuff on the floor and we'll pick it up!*

Wise for Salvation

Day 3. *ASK: Who is in our family? What makes up a family? What does our family do to help each other? What did Ruth do to help her family?*

Day 4. Have your child draw a picture of something from the story while you review it together. This story is quite long to read straight out of the Bible, but you may find it in a children's Bible.

Day 5. *ASK: How did Ruth show that she loved Naomi? How do you think Naomi felt when Ruth showed her this kind of love?*

PRAYER:

Thank you, God, for families. Help my family to be the best it can be, and help us all to love you like you love us.

Amen.

Ruth and Boaz

Ruth 2–4

Ruth went out to pick barley from a field so that she could feed herself and Naomi. The man who was in charge of the fields noticed her. He thought she was very brave for coming back to Bethlehem with Naomi, and he told her that she could pick barley from his field every day. His name was Boaz. Later, Boaz and Ruth got married and had a baby! Naomi and Ruth now had a family again.

Day 1. Read the paraphrase and/or act out the story with your child.

Day 2. Play Ring Around the Rosy with the following words: "God's love is amazing /We're singing and we're praising/We love others /Because he first loved us." *SAY: Our story is about love—the love Ruth had for Naomi, the love Boaz and Ruth had for each other, and most of all, the love God has for each one of us. We love others because God first loved us.*

Day 3. Show your children something made of grain. (Cereal, bread, oatmeal crackers, etc.) *ASK: Why do you think Ruth went out to collect grain? Was there anywhere else she could get food? So how did Ruth take care of Naomi?*

Wise for Salvation

Day 4. Help your child draw a picture of your family. Discuss each person, then pray for each family member individually.

Day 5. SAY: *Ruth, Naomi, and Boaz lived in a town named Bethlehem. Can you think of some other people who lived in Bethlehem?* (Both King David and Jesus were born in Bethlehem.)

PRAYER:

Thank you, God, for making a whole family out of a bunch of lonely people-Ruth, Noami, and Boaz. Please help our family to love and praise you like this family did.

Amen.

Hannah and Samuel

1 Samuel 1

Hannah loved God but was very sad because she had no children. One day she went to the temple to pray, and she asked God for a baby. She prayed so hard that she started crying, and a priest named Eli came to talk to her. He told her that God was going to answer her prayer, and he did! She had a baby and she named him Samuel. When he was still a little boy, she brought him to the temple to live and to serve the Lord with Eli.

Day 1. Read the paraphrase and/or act out the story with your child.

Day 2. ASK: How would you like to live at church with the pastor instead of at home with your family? What do you think would be fun about that? What would be sad about it?

Day 3. SAY: Hannah gave her son to God because she was so happy that God had answered her prayer for a baby. Have you ever prayed for something and had God say yes? Is there something we can pray about now?

Wise for Salvation

Day 4. While your child draws a picture of a baby, read the story straight from the Bible (1 Samuel 1:9–28), or a from a children's Bible.

Day 5. *SAY: God gives us all a family, just like he gave Hannah a family. Who is in our family? Talk about your immediate/extended family and then pray for them.*

PRAYER:

Thank you for showing Hannah that she could trust you, even when she thought she would never have a baby. Thank you for baby Samuel and all the wonderful works he did for you as he lived and worked in the temple.

Amen.

Samuel Hears God
1 Samuel 3:1–10

Samuel was a boy who lived in God's temple with Eli. One night, they were both asleep when someone called out, "Samuel!" Samuel ran over to Eli and said, "Here I am! Did you call me?" Eli was confused, because he hadn't called Samuel. He told him to go back to bed. Then God called Samuel again! "Samuel!" Again, Samuel jumped up and ran to Eli to help, but Eli hadn't called him. Samuel went back to bed, and it happened again! Finally, Eli figured out that it was God, so he told Samuel to speak to God the next time he called. Samuel went back to bed, and God called him again, "Samuel! Samuel!" This time, Samuel said, "Speak, your servant is listening," and God spoke to Samuel.

Day 1. Act out the story together.

Day 2. *ASK: If you heard your name in the middle of the night, what would you do? Would you think it was me?*

Wise for Salvation

Day 3. Have your child lie in bed and close their eyes. Whisper their name, then have them practice saying "Talk to me, God! I am listening!"

Day 4. Read the story straight from the Bible (1 Samuel 3:1–10) while your child draws a picture of Samuel sleeping.

Day 5. *SAY: Let's practice our listening skills by playing Simon Says!* Have your child do various activities, using your own ideas so they can be an appropriate energy level.

PRAYER:

Thank you, God, for speaking to Samuel. Please help us to listen to you too, whether it's while we're sleeping, when we're awake, or wherever we are. Help us to listen and obey.

Amen.

David Is Anointed

1 Samuel 16:1–13

God asked a man named Samuel to go and pour oil on the head of the man who would be the next king. But Samuel didn't know who it was supposed to be! He went to pick one of the sons of a man named Jesse. He looked at the first tall, strong, and handsome man, and thought, "Surely this man would make a great king!" But God told him that he was looking for someone with a heart that loved God. Finally, Samuel found David, who was just a shepherd boy. Nobody knew that a shepherd boy could turn out to be a king, but God knew! Samuel poured oil on his head and told him that someday he would be king of the whole country. That's a big job!

Day 1. Read the paraphrase together or act it out using yourselves or stuffed animals as characters. *SAY: Do you think Samuel thought it was weird that the little shepherd boy was going to be the king?*

Day 2. *SAY: When Samuel was looking for the king, seven men stood in front of him. Let's look at them all. Man #1 (point up with one finger), are you the kind of king God wants? Nope. Okay, Man #2, are you the kind of king God wants?* (Continue through the rest.) *Okay, Man #7, are you the kind of king God wants? No?! Then who's left? Oh, this smelly little shepherd boy. Hm. Okay, Boy #1, are YOU the kind of king that God wants? Oh, God says yes! I'm so glad that God has a plan.*

Wise for Salvation

Day 3. SAY: Many times when we go to the doctor, he can't tell if we have something wrong just by looking at us. We may look just fine on the outside, but there might be something wrong on the inside. To see what's on the inside, the doctor uses machines like x-rays and ultrasounds. By looking with the machine, he can see what's on the inside and helps us to get well. God does the same thing. He looks at our inside and wants us to have a healthy heart. What do you think is inside your heart?

Interactive option: pretend to be a patient while the doctor takes an x-ray of your heart!

Day 4. SAY: What do you think a king does all day? Do you think it's a hard job? Do you think God helped David when it was his turn to be king? What kind of hard jobs could you ask God to help you with?

Day 5. Read the story right out of the Bible (1 Samuel 16:1–13) while your child draws a picture of a king's crown.

PRAYER:

Thank you, God, for looking at who we really are, and not just looking at how strong we are or how good-looking we are. Help us to love you and to have hearts that are kind and beautiful.

Amen.

David Cares for His Sheep

1 Samuel 17:34–37

David was a shepherd. He cared for his sheep and wrote songs to God. David once told a story about what it was like to be a shepherd. He said that one time a big lion came roaring in and stole one of his sheep! He went after it, rescued the sheep, and killed the lion. A bear also tried to steal a sheep, but God helped David to protect his sheep from the bear too. David knew that God had helped him and protected him from the animals that wanted to hurt him and his sheep.

Day 1. Read the paraphrase together or act it out using yourselves or stuffed animals as characters. *SAY: Do you think David was scared when the lion and bear came to steal his sheep?*

Day 2. *SAY: As a shepherd, the sheep followed David wherever he went. Let's play "Follow the Leader" and pretend to be David and his sheep!*

Day 3. *SAY: David had a whole bunch of sheep to take care of. Do you have an animal that you take care of? How do you take care of it?* (If you don't have a pet, talk about how you can show kindness to an animal this week.)

Day 4. David learned how to be a good shepherd from God. The Bible says that God is like our shepherd. Together with your child, pretend to be a shepherd and a sheep as you read the following excerpts from Psalm 23:

"The Lord is my shepherd, I do not need anything."
"He makes me lie down in green pastures."
"He brings me beside quiet water to drink."

ASK: How does God do these things for us?

Day 5. As you read 1 Samuel 17:37, have your child draw their version of God being with them when they're scared. *SAY: David knows that God will help him and protect him against a big giant because God helped him and protected him against the lion and the bear. Where has God helped you or protected you?*

PRAYER:

Thank you, God, for helping David take good care of his sheep! Please help me trust you when I am afraid.

Amen.

David and Goliath

1 Samuel 17:1–50

There was a big bad army that had a big bad man named Goliath in it. This big bad man made fun of God and God's people and tried to hurt them. David the shepherd boy decided that this needed to end. He picked up a stone, put it in his sling, then whipped the sling around over his head. When he let it go, the sling let loose an itty-bitty stone which flew into the giant's big, mean, round head and knocked him down! With God's help, even little people can defeat giants.

Note: If you'd like to read the story to your child, the actual showdown is found in 1 Samuel 17:40–50. However, please proofread it before reading to your child, as it contains some very graphic language!

Day 1. Find the biggest stuffed animal you have in the house and the smallest. Pretend that they are David and Goliath. *SAY: What did Goliath say to David? What did David say to Goliath? What did David do? Do you think David was scared?*

Day 2. Find something small and soft, like a cotton ball or a small stuffed animal. Have your child throw it at you to see if they can knock you down. *ASK: Why do you think you couldn't knock me down? How do you think David knocked down Goliath with just a small rock? Do you think he had help from someone?*

Day 3. Draw a picture of David and Goliath together while talking about the story. *SAY: I wonder how Goliath felt when he saw that stone coming towards his face!*

Day 4. Practice memorizing the following verse while pretending to swing a sling. When you say "possible," let the pretend sling fly! *"With God all things are possible"* (Matthew 19:26, NIV)

Day 5. *SAY: There are lots of things in our lives that can seem really big and scary. Is there something that seems really scary to you right now? Something that you're afraid of?* Read David's words in 1 Samuel 17:47. *Who is the one who protects us? Let's ask God right now to save you from what is scaring you.*

PRAYER:

Thank you, God, for helping David take down the big mean giant. You are bigger than any problem. Help me to remember to ask you for help when I have questions or issues.

Amen.

David and Jonathan

1 Samuel 18:3–4

Jonathan was a prince, and his dad was the king of Israel: King Saul. There was a boy that King Saul really didn't like, and that boy's name was David. But guess who thought David was pretty cool? That's right, Prince Jonathan! Prince Jonathan wanted to be David's friend, so they made a promise to each other to love each other as friends. To show David that he was telling the truth, Prince Jonathan gave David some of his clothes, his bow and arrow, and his belt.

Day 1. Read the paraphrase and/or act out the story of David and Jonathan's pact with your child.

Day 2. ASK: Who are your friends? What do you like to do with your friends? What do you do to show your friends that you love them?

Day 3. ASK: What did Jonathon give to David to show that they were friends? Can you think of something you could give to one of your friends?

Day 4. Read the verses from the Bible while your child draws a picture of them and a friend playing together.

Day 5. Cut out (or tear) a few long strips of a piece of paper. Tape or staple them together to fit your child around the waist, like the belt Jonathan gave to David. On it, write the following verse: *"Be kind to one another…"* (Ephesians 4:32, ESV)

Help your child put the belt on, then ask them about what it says on the belt. You can ask it in different ways, or be silly and pretend that you keep forgetting. In this way, you will help your child memorize the verse!

PRAYER:

Thank you, God, for friends. Help me to learn how to be a friend and to find good friends to be with me in my life.

Amen.

Elijah Fed by Ravens

1 Kings 17:1–6

The king of Israel was a bad man, and he didn't like God's friend Elijah very much. So God told Elijah to go into hiding for a while. He camped out by a brook, and every day God sent ravens to feed him—they brought him bread and meat for breakfast, and bread and meat for supper every day. God took care of his friend Elijah.

Day 1. Read the paraphrase together or act it out using yourselves or some stuffed birds as characters. *SAY: Do you think Elijah was scared to go out in the wilderness where there wasn't any food?*

Day 2. Pretend to be a raven getting a message from God about bringing food to Elijah. What does God tell you? Where do you get the food from? How do you know where to find Elijah?

Day 3. Read 1 Kings 17:1–6 while your child draws a picture of a bird. *SAY: Why do you think God sent food for Elijah?*

Day 4. *SAY: 1 Kings 17:5 says that Elijah did as the Lord told him, even though God told him to go hide in a strange place. God was able to meet all of Elijah's needs because Elijah obeyed God.* Pray together, asking God that he would meet your needs, and that you would be brave enough to obey whatever he asks.

Day 5. Flap your wings like a raven and practice memorizing a verse: *"And my God will meet all your needs…"* (Philippians 4:19, NIV) *SAY: How has God met your needs today?*

PRAYER:

Thank you, God, for meeting the needs of Elijah, for giving him water and food and a safe place to stay. We trust you that you will meet our needs as well. Thank you!

Amen.

Elijah and the Widow

1 Kings 17:7–16

Because there was no rain for a long time, the brook where Elijah was hiding dried up. God told him to go to a different town and live with a woman and her son. The lady didn't want to give Elijah any food, because she had only a tiny little bit left and she was afraid that her and her son would starve. Elijah told her that if she shared with him, God promised that her jar of flour would never be used up and her jug of oil would not run dry. So she shared her food with him, and God saved the woman, her son, and Elijah from starvation.

Day 1. Read the paraphrase together or act it out using yourselves as characters! *ASK: Do you think the woman was afraid to share her last little bit of food with Elijah?*

Day 2. *SAY: Both the widow and Elijah showed obedience to God. Elijah went to the town and the widow gave him bread. God was able to meet all of Elijah's needs and the widow's needs because they obeyed God.* Pray together, asking God that he would meet your needs, and that you would be brave enough to obey whatever he asks.

Day 3. Read 1 Kings 17:7–16 while your child draws a picture of bread. *SAY: Did God keep his promise to Elijah and the widow? Our God keeps his promises!*

Day 4. Show your child a container that might pass as a jar of flour or a jug of oil (such as a mason jar or a plastic food container). *SAY: Do you see the bottom of this? If I filled it up, then kept using it, would you see the bottom again? God promised that the widow's jar of flour and jug of oil would never get used up if she obeyed him, and he kept his promise. It was a miracle!*

Day 5. Practice memorizing the following verse in two different ways—the first as if you are starving, and the second as if God has filled up your tummies with good bread: *"And my God will meet all your needs…"* (Philippians 4:19, NIV) *SAY: How has God met our family's needs today?*

PRAYER:

Thank you, God, for meeting our needs. Help us to remember to trust you for everything, including the food we eat. Thank you that you love us and take care of us.

Amen.

Elijah on Mount Carmel
1 Kings 18:1–39

God's people had forgotten about him and started worshipping a statue; they thought that it was God and that it could hear them. God didn't like this, so he sent Elijah to show them that they were wrong. Elijah arranged a contest. Each group was supposed to set up an altar with an animal on it, and whoever sent fire from heaven to burn up the altar was the one true God. The people who worshipped the statue called to it all day, but it couldn't hear them—it couldn't send down fire from heaven because it was a piece of rock. But then Elijah prayed. He asked God to show the people that he is God, so they would start to love God again. And God did something amazing: he sent down a huge fire from heaven—whoosh—that burned up everything on the altar! Then God's people remembered him and worshipped him.

Day 1. Read the paraphrase and/or act out the story together.

Day 2. Read 1 Kings 18:26, 29. *SAY: Why do you think no one answered these guys? Were they praying to the real God?*

Day 3. Read 1 Kings 18:30–35. *SAY: Why do you think Elijah wanted them to put so much water on? Do you think that much water would make it hard for God to make a fire there?*

Day 4. Read 1 Kings 18:36–39. *SAY: Wow. Do you think the people were surprised that the fire came down and burned up even the water? I bet they were! God sure knows how to show people that he's God!*

Day 5. *SAY: God did this whole contest to have his people remember one thing: "The Lord—he is God!" (1 Kings 18:39) The people were so surprised that God had done such an amazing thing that they actually fell down on their faces and worshipped God. Let's try that. Together, lay facedown on the ground and say, "The Lord—he is God!"*

PRAYER:

God, you are so amazing! You are the only real and true God, and you listen to us when we call on you. Help us to always worship only you.

Amen.

Elijah Listens to God
1 Kings 19:9–13

Elijah was very sad—lots of people were running away from God, and he felt like he was the only one left who loved God. He went out to a cave on a mountain to complain to God. While he was there, God promised to pass by. Then a great and powerful wind tore the mountains apart and broke rocks, but God was not in the great wind. After the wind there was an earthquake that shook the mountain, but God was not in the earthquake. After the earthquake came a crackling fire, but God was not in the fire. After the fire came a gentle whisper. When Elijah heard it, he pulled his coat over his face and went out of the cave. And God spoke to him in a gentle whisper.

Day 1. Act out the story with lots of dramatic effects!

Day 2. *SAY: Elijah went to the cave because he was sad that everyone was running away from God. Are there some things that make you sad? Talk to God about them now. At the end, ask God to whisper to your heart. Is there anything you want to say to me, God?*

Christie Thomas

Day 3. *SAY: Let's practice listening to very quiet things by whispering secrets to each other.* Whisper things like "God loves you" and "Jesus wants to be your friend forever" into your child's ear.

Day 4. Be very quiet and listen to the sounds around you. What do you hear? *ASK: Why do you think God decided to talk to Elijah in a whisper instead of in a big loud voice?*

Day 5. Read the story straight from the Bible (1 Kings 19:11–13) while your child draws a picture of a cave.

PRAYER:

God, thank you for making the great and powerful things like winds and fires, and thank you for making quiet things like whispers. Help us to hear your whispering in our hearts. Help our hearts and minds to be quiet enough to hear you.

Amen.

Elisha and the Widow
2 Kings 4:1–7

A friend of Elisha's had died, and the man's wife was very sad because she had no money for her and her two boys. Elisha told her to go find every empty jar she could possibly find—she was even supposed to ask her neighbours for jars! Once her house was full of jars, Elisha told her to pour oil from her little container into the jars. She poured and poured and poured, but the little jar of oil didn't run out of oil until the last big jar had been filled. It was a miracle! Then the lady was able to sell all the jars of oil and have money for her family.

Day 1. Act out the story together and/or read the paraphrase.

Day 2. Get a bottle of cooking oil from the kitchen. Show your child the bottle. *ASK: What would happen if I poured this out? Would the jug be full? No, it would be empty! So when Elisha asked the woman to keep pouring oil from her little jug into all those jars, what do you think she thought? Do you think she might have been worried if there would be enough oil? Isn't it amazing how God met the needs of this woman?*

Day 3. Talk about a difficulty that is facing your child right now. Perhaps there is trouble in school, sadness over a favourite pet, a friend moving away, or family sickness. *SAY: How does that make you feel? Where do you go when you feel sad, or angry, or all alone? The woman in this story went to Elisha, God's friend, because she knew that God would help her, through Elisha. Let's ask God to help us too.*

Day 4. Read the story straight from the Bible 2 Kings 4:1–7, while your child draws a picture of a jar. *SAY: God helped the woman, but she had to also obey God. If she hadn't gotten the jars, poured in the oil, and sold the oil, the miracle would not have happened. Is there some way that we can also show obedience to God today?*

Day 5. *SAY: God used Elisha to help the widow. Sometimes God wants to use us to help others in need as well. Perhaps someone might like an encouragement card, or a meal. What could we make together this weekend to help this person?* Decide on something you can do together, then bless someone this weekend!

Wise for Salvation

PRAYER:

God, thank you so much for meeting the widow's needs. Thank you for promising to meet all of our needs. Help us to bring our needs to you every day and allow you to meet them in your own amazing way.

Amen.

Naaman

2 Kings 5:1–3, 9–14

Naaman was an important man, but he had a very bad sickness called leprosy. In his house worked a servant girl who knew about God's friend Elisha, and she told Naaman that Elisha could heal him. So off he went on a trip to find Elisha. When he came to Elisha's house, Elisha sent out a messenger telling him to go wash himself seven times in the Jordan River. Naaman was *so* mad because he thought this was a terrible way to get healed. The Jordan River was not exactly a clean place. He thought that Elisha should just come out and wave his hands over him instead of making him wash in dirty water! But God was waiting to see if Naaman would be humble and follow his instructions. Finally, Naaman did what Elisha said, and God healed him of his leprosy. After that, he decided that he would become a follower of God!

Day 1. Act out the story together and/or read the paraphrase. *ASK: What is your favourite part of this story?*

Day 2. Go to a tap and put your hands in the water seven times. *ASK: How did that feel? Did it feel kind of silly to do the same thing seven times? How did Naaman feel about what Elisha asked him to do? Has your mom or dad ever asked you to do something that you thought was silly, but was actually really important?*

Wise for Salvation

Day 3. Read the story straight from the Bible, 2 Kings 5:1–3, 9–14 while your child draws a picture of a river. *ASK: Is it always easy to obey when someone gives us instructions? No way, it sure isn't always easy! What did God want Naaman to do? And what happened when Naaman actually did it?*

Day 4. Practice memorizing the following verse by saying it in two different ways. First, pretend to be sick like Naaman was. Say together: *"And my God will meet all your needs…"* (Philippians 4:19, NIV) Then pretend to go into the river and dip in seven times. Afterward, recite the verse again! God sure does meet our needs!

Day 5. *SAY: Do we know someone who is sick? They probably don't have leprosy like Naaman, but they still need to know that God loves them. Let's pray for him/her today.*

PRAYER:

Thank you, God, for healing Naaman, and for teaching him to follow you at the same time! Help us to remember that you meet all our needs!

Amen.

Esther, the Queen who Saved God's People

Esther

Most children have only heard small parts of the story of Esther. During this week's devotions, we'll go through the whole thing so they can find out how God was with Esther! Each day, have your child either draw that part of the story as you read, or role-play it with them.

Day 1. Esther is chosen. The king needed a new queen. He sent his servants out into all his kingdom and had them bring back a whole bunch of girls so he could meet them. The girls spent a whole year having beauty treatments before they even got to meet the king! One of the girls was named Esther, and she was one of God's special people, called the Jews. Lots of the girls wanted to be queen, but the king chose Esther, because he liked her the best. He was so excited when he met her that he put the crown on her head and declared her queen. To celebrate, he had a huge party! *ASK: What kind of person do you think makes a good king or queen?*

Day 2. Haman hatches a plot. There was a really bad guy in the kingdom, and his name was Haman. The king didn't know he was a really bad guy, so he put him in charge of lots of important things. Haman really hated the Jews, so he decided to trick the king into having them all killed. Killed! What a really bad guy. And his plan worked! He tricked the king into making a law that said all the Jews had to die. *ASK: How would you feel if someone tricked you into doing something really bad?*

Day 3. Esther goes to the king. Esther found out about Haman's plan, and she was so scared, because the new law meant that she and all her family would have to die. Yikes! She decided to talk to the king. This was a scary thing to do, because this king didn't like people talking to him unless he invited them into his throne room. If they walked in without being invited, the king was allowed to throw them in jail! And Queen Esther hadn't been invited. So first, she prayed to God that he would make her brave. Then she got her fanciest dress on and walked into the throne room. When the king saw Queen Esther standing there, he held out his gold sceptre, which meant that she was allowed to come in. The king asked her, "What do you want, Queen Esther? What is your request? I will give it to you, even if it is half the kingdom!" *ASK: What would you ask for if the king told you that you were allowed to ask for anything you wanted?*

Day 4. Esther has a party. When the king asked Esther what she wanted, she told him that all she wanted was for him and Haman to come to a party! Of course, they were quite excited about this. Then she invited them to another party! At this second party, the king finally asked her what she actually wanted. She told him that a really bad guy was trying to kill her and her people, and that she wanted the king to save her. The king was shocked! Who could be wanting to kill his wonderful queen? Esther pointed at Haman, and said, "This wicked Haman is our enemy." Then the king finally figured out that he had been tricked by the really bad guy. He got rid of Haman and saved the Jews. Hooray! *ASK: How would you feel if someone saved your life?*

Day 5. *SAY: Think of some times in Esther's story when she had to be brave. In Matthew 28:20, God says, "I am with you always…" (NIV) How do you think God helped Esther?*

PRAYER:

Thank you, God, for being with Esther and for giving her courage. Thank you for making her the queen so she was able to save the Jews. You think of everything, God! Help us to trust you like Esther trusted you.

Amen.

Daniel Prays

Daniel 6

Daniel worked for a king. He was very good at his job and the king really liked him. But the king's other helpers didn't like Daniel, because they were jealous of him. So they decided to trick the king into making a rule that people were only allowed to pray to the king, instead of to God. The king thought that would be a *great* rule, because he liked feeling special. Daniel did not think it was a great rule, so he went to his room and prayed to God anyway. The king's helpers tattled on him and the king had to follow his own rule and throw Daniel into a cave full of hungry lions! Oh no! Everyone thought the lions would gobble Daniel up, but God saved Daniel. In the morning, everyone was very surprised that Daniel was still alive. God had shut the mouths of the lions! The king took Daniel out of the cave and was so very happy that God had saved him.

Day 1. After reading the story to your child, act it out together.

Day 2. SAY: *Daniel prayed to God even though it was against the rules. Did you know that there are still some places in the world where it's against the rules to pray to God? Let's talk to God right now. We'll thank him that it's not against the rules to pray in our country, and we'll pray that people in other countries would have courage like Daniel to keep talking to God.*

Day 3. Read the story directly from the Bible (Daniel 6:6–7, 10, 16–23) while your child draws a picture of a lion.

Day 4. Pretend to be the hungry lions in the cave. Imagine that some tasty food gets dropped in. *ASK: What happened to the lions when Daniel got dropped in?* (Daniel 6:22) Pretend to be the lions after the angel has shut their mouths. How do you think they acted?

Day 5. Practice memorizing a Bible verse while roaring like lions, with your mouths closed, and while jumping for joy: *"I am with you always…"* (Matthew 28:20, NIV)

PRAYER:

Thank you, God, for giving Daniel the courage to pray even when he knew it was against the rules. Thank you for saving him from the lions and for teaching the king that we should only pray to you, not to people.

Amen.

Three Brave Men
Daniel 3

The king had made a giant statue out of metal, and he thought that it was God. He made a rule that everyone had to bow down before the statue, or else they would be thrown into a fire. Most people obeyed and bowed down to the statue, but there were three men who would not. Shadrach, Meshach, and Abednego refused to bow down to the statue because they knew the real God wouldn't like that. The king got *super* angry, and he told the soldiers to throw the three men into a fiery furnace! It was so hot that even the soldiers who threw them into the fire got burnt. But not Shadrach, Meshach, and Abednego! The king peered into the fire and was very surprised to see the men walking around, definitely not dead! And he was even more surprised that there were four men in the fire, not three. He called them out, and the three men stepped out of the fire. They were not burned at all.

Day 1. After reading the story to your kids, act it out together.

Day 2. Read Daniel 3:28 to find out who the king thought Man #4 in the furnace was. *ASK: Do you think he was right? Who else might it have been?* Practice memorizing the following verse from the Bible: *"I am with you always…"* (Matthew 28:20, NIV)

Day 3. Read the story directly from the Bible (Daniel 3:13, 14, 20–27) while your child draws a picture of a fire.

Day 4. Read what the king says about God after seeing the great rescue: "There is no other god who can rescue like this!" Do you know someone who needs rescuing? (Perhaps from an illness, a situation, or from being far from God.) Pray together. *SAY: God, we know that there is no one else who can rescue like you. Please rescue _____ from _____.*

Day 5. *SAY: Shadrach, Meshach, and Abednego obeyed God's rule about only bowing to him instead of the king's rule about bowing down to the statue. Can you think of a time when you chose to obey God? How do you know what God's rules are?*

PRAYER:

Thank you, God, for saving Shadrach, Meshach, and Abednego. Thank you for helping them follow you and then saving them. Thank you for showing everyone that you are the God who rescues.

Amen.

Jonah the Runaway Prophet

Jonah 1–2

God asked Jonah to go tell some bad people that he wasn't very impressed with their behaviour. Jonah didn't want to do it, so he ran away and jumped on a boat. He thought he could hide from God. But God knew where he was and sent a big storm after him. The sailors on the boat were scared, so Jonah told them to throw him into the sea! Jonah fell into the water and thought he was going to die, but God saved Jonah by sending a big fish to swallow him down. Gulp! After three days in the fish, Jonah told God that we was sorry for running away, and he promised to do what God had asked. So God had the fish spit Jonah out onto a beach. And right away, Jonah went and obeyed God!

Day 1. Read the paraphrase and/or act out the story with your child.

Day 2. *SAY: Jonah tried to hide from God. Do you think that's a good idea? Let's see if we can think of some place in our house where God couldn't find us. Hmmm, I can't think of any, can you? Do you think God knew where Jonah was?* (If you have time, play a game of hide-and-seek with your child and remind them that God is always with them!)

Day 3. Put some water in a sink or a large bowl and encourage your child to blow bubbles in the bowl, either with a straw or by sticking their face in. *ASK: How would you feel if you got tossed in the ocean and didn't know how to swim? Do you think Jonah knew that the fish was going to swallow him?*

Day 4. Go find the stinkiest garbage can in your house and have your child sniff it. *SAY: The inside of a fish is not a nice place to be! It might smell a little bit like this garbage can. Ew! Let's imagine that we're inside the fish with Jonah. What can we see/smell/taste/touch/hear?*

Day 5. *SAY: In the end, Jonah repented and did what God had asked him to do. "Repented" means that he said that he was sorry and that he wouldn't disobey again. Is there something that you need to repent of, or someone that you need to say sorry to?*

PRAYER:

Thank you, God, for showing Jonah that your way really is the best way! Help us to trust and obey you always.

Amen.

Christmas

After Christmas this year, my eldest announced, "Mom, Christmas really is about the presents…" I waited with bated breath for the rest of the sentence: "…because God gave us Jesus!" Phew!

I realize that Christmas is a confusing time for a lot of Christian parents. We want to join in all the fun with elves on shelves and the expectation of Santa and his mountain of gifts. Sometimes we feel that maybe the story about the baby in the stable isn't extraordinary enough, not magical enough to give our kids the same kind of Christmas memories we have from childhood.

So what is a parent to do? How can we make the Christ part of Christmas exciting and relevant for our little ones?

The following devotions contain a few of many ways to help your children remember that it's not just about the presents and Santa and elves on shelves. The Christ part of Christmas doesn't have to be boring! We can make new Christmas traditions, ones full of joy and laughter, ones with extraordinary magic because of their eternal basis.

Traditions like lighting advent candles, having toy Wise Men chase a star around one's house, choosing gifts for others out of charity catalogues, and making biblically themed crafts can make the season of advent and Christmas incredibly fun, and maybe even more marvelous than the ones you fondly remember from your own childhood.

This Christmas, my three-year-old encountered the Christmas story for the first time in his memory. When we visited my in-laws at the beginning of December, he paid no heed to the beautiful crèche they had displayed. During his next visit three weeks later, he very excitedly told me, "Grandma and Grandpa have a stable!" Somewhere in those intervening three weeks, something had clicked and the birth of Jesus had become extraordinary and magical to him.

An Angel Visits Mary
Luke 1:26–33, 38

One day, a girl named Mary was hanging out, probably doing some laundry. Suddenly, something super bright was standing right in front of her! She freaked out a bit, but the shiny thing turned out to be an angel from God. He told her that God had chosen her to do something very special. He said that God wanted Mary to have a baby, even though she wasn't married yet. She was pretty confused, but God said that he really wanted *her* to have this baby. See, this baby wasn't just any old baby. It was God's own Son. This baby was going to be the Saviour! God had chosen Mary for a very special job—she would get to be the mom of God's Son, and she was supposed to call him Jesus.

Day 1. Mary would have been very excited about the birth of her Son, just as we get excited to celebrate his birthday. With your child, put together a paper chain with one link for each day before Christmas. Remember to take off one link each day! *ASK: Are you excited about Christmas? Why?*

Day 2. Act out the story together, with one person being Mary and one being the angel. Mary could be doing chores when the angel surprises her with some amazing news. Put your emotions into it and really imagine how you might feel if an angel visited you.

Wise for Salvation

Day 3. Read this part of the story in a children's Bible. *ASK: What's your favourite part of the story? Why?*

Day 4. Have your child draw a picture of an angel while you read Luke 1:26–33, 38. *ASK: How do you think Mary felt when the angel appeared?*

Day 5. Mary reacted to this good news by writing a worship song. Together with your child, write a song or poem of worship to God.

PRAYER:

God, thank you for choosing Mary, an ordinary person, to be the mommy of your Son. Thank you for loving the world so much that you sent your Son to live with us. Help us to remember that you are the reason we have Christmas!

Amen.

Jesus Is Born

Luke 2:1–7

Just before Mary had her baby, the king decided that he wanted everyone in the country to be counted and pay taxes, but they had to be in their hometown. So Mary and Joseph left their town and went to Bethlehem, which is where Joseph's family was from. While they were there, Mary had her baby. Sadly, since there were so many people in Bethlehem, there was no room in anyone's house for them to sleep in. But someone did let them stay with the animals. Only the newborn Saviour ended up with a bed that night, and it was a manger—that is where people kept the food for their animals! And they called him Jesus, just as the angel had said.

Day 1. Pretend that you are Mary and Joseph and take a long walk through your home. When you reach your child's bedroom, shut the door and say, "There's no room here! I guess we'll have to rest in the hallway." *ASK: What do you think it was like for Mary to go on a long trip with a baby in her tummy? How does it feel to be told that there's no room for you?*

Day 2. Find a nativity scene and use it to re-enact the story. *ASK: What do you like the best about the story?*

Wise for Salvation

Day 3. Have your child draw a picture of a baby while you read Luke 2:1–7. *ASK: Why do you think Mary wrapped him up? How do we take care of babies in our country?*

Day 4. Pretend to be barn/stable animals together. *ASK: Where do women normally have babies? Do you think Mary was surprised to have her baby in the barn? How do you think it smelled? Was it warm or cold? Do you think Mary was scared? Why or why not?* Sing "Away in a Manger" together.

Day 5. Find a baby doll or a stuffed animal and a box or laundry basket. Put the doll in the basket, pretending that it is baby Jesus in the manger. Gather around the box, then pray: *Thank you so much, Jesus, for coming, and for being born in a barn instead of in a castle. Thank you for loving so much that you would come down from heaven to live with us. We love you so much, Jesus.*

PRAYER:

Thank you, God, for protecting Mary and Joseph on their long trip. And we most especially thank you for the gift of your Son, Jesus.

Amen.

Shepherds Hear Some Great News

Luke 2:8–20

One dark and quiet night, some shepherds were watching their sheep in a field. Suddenly, there was a bright light and an angel spoke to them! The angel said that there was an extra special baby who had just been born, and that they should go visit him. The baby's name was Jesus. Then even more angels joined the first one and they sang praises to God. After they left, the sky grew dark and the field became quiet again. The shepherds were so excited that they jumped up and ran to Bethlehem to see baby Jesus. After they saw him, they told everyone they knew that Jesus had been born!

Day 1. Pretend that you are shepherds taking care of sheep. *ASK: What do shepherds do for their sheep? What do they do when the sheep are hungry? Thirsty? Tired?* Jesus says that he is like our shepherd and he takes care of us like the shepherds took care of their sheep.

Day 2. Turn off the lights in your room and have your child pretend to be sleeping. Suddenly, turn on the lights or a bright flashlight and tell your child what the angel said. *ASK: Did I surprise you? How do you think the shepherds felt when the angel showed up?* Sing "Angels We Have Heard on High," or another angel Christmas carol, with your child.

96

Wise for Salvation

Day 3. After the shepherds heard about Jesus' birth, they had to go find him. Hide a small doll or stuffed animal and have your child go find "baby Jesus." *ASK: How do you think the shepherds felt when they found the baby? How would you feel if you got to see the real baby Jesus?*

Day 4. Draw the shape of a shepherd's staff (with a crook). Show your child the similarity between the candy cane shape and the shepherd's staff. *SAY: The man who invented the candy cane made it in the shape of a shepherd's staff to remind us that shepherds visited the baby Jesus at his birth! If we look at the candy cane upside-down, what letter does it look like? A "J"! And whose name starts with J? Jesus!*

Day 5. Read this part of the Christmas story in a children's Bible. *ASK: I wonder why God showed these shepherds how to find Jesus. What made them so special that they got to meet God's Son?*

PRAYER:

Thank you, God, for telling your great news to ordinary people. Thank you for loving the world so much that you sent your Son. Help us to remember you and the best present of all this Christmas.

Amen.

Wise Men Meet Jesus

Matthew 2:1–11

When Jesus was born, people noticed that there was a beautiful star shining brightly in the sky. Some wise men from far away saw the star and knew that it meant a new king had been born. They packed up some camping supplies and went on the long journey to find the baby king. They followed the star right to the place where baby Jesus was living. When they saw him, they bowed down and worshipped him, and gave him wonderful gifts.

Day 1. Pretend to be the wise men and go on a little journey through your house, looking for baby Jesus. *ASK: How do you think the wise men felt on their long trip? What did they think when they finally found the baby they were looking for? Do you think they were surprised that the baby king wasn't living in a castle?*

Day 2. *SAY: Do you remember what the wise men followed to find the baby Jesus? Let's sing "Twinkle, Twinkle, Little Star" together to remind us about the amazing thing God put in the sky when Jesus was born!*

Day 3. Have your child draw a picture of a star while you read Matthew 2:1–11. *ASK: Have you ever been on a long journey? What would you bring with you if you were going to find a newborn baby?*

Day 4. Read today's story in a children's Bible. *ASK: I wonder why God showed these men how to find Jesus. What made them so special that they got to meet God's Son?*

Day 5. *SAY: The wise men brought baby Jesus some interesting gifts—gold, frankincense, and myrrh. Frankincense and myrrh are types of perfume. What kind of gift would you bring the baby Jesus?*

Option for families with multiple children: Have your child choose one of their special toys, which they can gift to another child in the family. *ASK: Why do we give gifts at Christmas? What makes a good gift?*

PRAYER:

God, you are so amazing to be able to put a star in the sky for people from another country to follow. Thank you for showing these strangers the baby Jesus. Thank you that you care about and love everyone.

Amen.

The Life of Jesus

Here he is: the crux of God's great, millennia-spanning plan of salvation!

- Jesus, the compelling leader.
- Jesus, the intelligent teacher.
- Jesus, the complex theologian.
- Jesus, the stopper of storms.
- Jesus, the fondest friend.
- Jesus, the patient forgiver.
- Jesus, the magnificent healer.
- Jesus, the unblemished Passover lamb.

May you and your child fall in love with Jesus as you experience his life and teachings!

Jesus Obeys His Father
Luke 2:41–50

When Jesus was a big kid, his family travelled a long way to Jerusalem for a big party called the Passover. But when they left, Jesus stayed behind! His parents searched and searched for three whole days. They were worried that they would never find him. Finally, they looked in the temple, and there he was! He was teaching the adults about God. His parents were kind of angry with him, but He told them that he was being obedient to his Father in heaven. God wanted Jesus to teach others about him, and Jesus was obeying.

Day 1. While you read Luke 2:41–50, have your child draw a squiggly line around the paper showing all the places that Mary and Joseph looked for Jesus. *ASK: How do you think Jesus' parents felt when they lost him? How do you think they felt when they found him?*

Day 2. Act out the story with your child, or have some dolls or stuffed animals act it out for you. See how much your child can tell you from memory. *SAY: What is your favourite part of this story? Why?*

Day 3. *ASK: Have you ever been lost somewhere and didn't know where your parents were?* (If not, help your child imagine a situation in which they are lost in a grocery store or in the middle of a big crowd.) *How did you feel? Do you think Jesus felt scared or not?*

Day 4. *SAY: When Jesus' parents found him, what was Jesus doing? When Jesus talked about God with the people in the temple, he was doing what God wanted him to do. When we obey God like Jesus did, we show love to him. How do you show love to God?*

Day 5. *Read Luke 2:52. SAY: Jesus was able to grow in favour with God and people because he knew God's word. Let's practice memorizing this verse together: "Loving God means obeying his commands" (1 John 5:3, NCV).*

PRAYER:

Dear Jesus, you are so amazing. Thank you for showing us how to love God—by telling everyone about your word and by obeying you. Help us to love you and obey you.

Amen.

Two Important Rules
Matthew 22:34–39

Some of the leaders of Israel got together and asked Jesus a question. They asked, "Which is the most important rule in the Bible?" Jesus answered them: *"'Love the Lord your God with all your heart and with all your soul and with all your mind.' This is the first and greatest commandment. And the second is like it: 'Love your neighbor as yourself'"* (Matthew 22:37–39, NIV).

Day 1. Read Matthew 22:34–39 right out of the Bible. *SAY: Do you remember what the two most important rules are that Jesus gave? Love God and love other people.* Help your child draw a picture of a heart to remind them that God's most important rules are about love.

Day 2. *SAY: The first and most important rule is to love God. Let's make a Valentine's card for God!* Help your child write "I love you, God" or something similar from their heart. Post it in their room to remind them about how they love God!

Day 3. Re-enact the story with your child, with you asking the questions posed by the leaders and with your child pretending to be Jesus. See how much of Jesus' answer your child can remember! Prompt as much as necessary. *SAY: If you got to make up any rule for the whole world, what would your rule be? What do you think the leaders thought of Jesus' rule?*

Day 4. *SAY: The second rule that Jesus talks about is to love your neighbour. Who is your neighbour?* (Most preschoolers will take this literally to mean the person who lives next door. Go with that for now, as there will be opportunities to teach the more abstract meaning of the word in other devotions.) *What can we do to love our neighbour today?* (You could make a card for your neighbour, or plan to do something nice the next day.)

Day 5. *SAY: How can we show love to God today?* (Together, think of something your child can do that would honour God. Perhaps it would be singing "Jesus Loves Me" or practicing the memory verse. Let your child come up with the answer!)

PRAYER:

Dear God, we love you so much. Please help us to love you and to love our neighbours.

Amen.

How to Pray
Matthew 6:5–13

Jesus teaches us about prayer. He tells us to pray to God without worrying about what other people think, and to pray what is really important to us, not pretend words that don't mean anything. Then he gives us an example of a prayer. We will go through that prayer this week.

Day 1. Read Matthew 6:9–10, paraphrased: "You are our Great Big God. Please be in charge of the world just like you're already in charge of heaven." *SAY: When we tell God that he is our Great Big God, that is a way of saying "I praise you." What are some other things you could say to God? What do you like best about God? What's really cool about him?* Draw/write these things onto a piece of paper, and write "I praise you" at the top.

Day 2. Read Matthew 6:11, paraphrased: "Please give us the things we need every day." *SAY: God tells us that he wants to answer our prayers. What are some things you could ask God to help you with today?* Draw/write these things onto a piece of paper, and write "Help me" at the top.

Day 3. Read Matthew 6:12–13, paraphrased: "Please forgive us for the bad things we've done and help us forgive people who have done bad things to us. Help us to be good." *SAY: When we do something bad, something that hurts someone else, we have to apologize to them. But we also need to apologize to God, because when we do bad things, it hurts God's heart. What is something you can apologize to God for?* Draw/write these things onto a piece of paper, and write "I'm sorry" at the top.

Day 4. *SAY: Colossians 3:15 says "Be thankful." God tells us a lot of times in the Bible that we need to thank him for what he's given us and done for us. What is something that you enjoyed today that you can thank God for?* Draw/write these things onto a piece of paper, and write "Thank you" at the top.

Day 5. Today, try to do all four sections of the prayer: I praise you, Help me, I'm sorry, and Thank you. Continue to use this routine whenever you pray with your child to help them understand the different aspects of prayer.

Good Samaritan

Luke 10:25–37

A man asked Jesus about the most important rules, and Jesus said, "Love God and love others." The man wondered who he was supposed to love, and Jesus told him a story about a man.

The man was walking from one town to another when some robbers beat him up and stole everything from him. He was very badly hurt, but no one would stop to help him. The important people would not stop to help him, and the holy people would not stop to help him. But someone who he didn't like stopped to help him. The man, called a Samaritan, picked him up, put bandages on him, and brought him somewhere where he could get better.

Jesus said that this is who we are supposed to love: everyone, no matter who they are.

Day 1. Read Luke 10:30–35 while your child draws a picture of a Band-Aid. *ASK: How does it make you feel when two people walk right by the hurt man and don't help him? Why? How do you think the man felt when he had to wait a long time to get help? How do you think God wants us to help others this week?*

Day 2. Read Luke 10:27–29 and 36–37. *ASK: Who is your neighbour? God tells us that loving our neighbour doesn't just mean loving the people who live next door; it means loving everyone. Let's think of three people you can show love to today.*

Day 3. Act out the story with your child, with one of you pretending to be the robbed man and the other(s) being the other characters. *ASK: What do you think God likes best about this story? What does this story teach us about God?*

Day 4. Read Luke 10:31–32. *ASK: Why do you think those two men ignored the guy who was hurt? Do we sometimes ignore others when they are hurt? Why?* Together, pray that God would help you see those who need help, and give you courage to help them.

Day 5. Act out some scenarios of someone needing help, and help your child to think of a way they could help the person.

- You fell off a bike and hurt yourself.
- You are sad.
- You are in a bad mood.
- You are very hungry and don't have any food.

PRAYER:

Thank you, God, for loving everyone, not just the people who love you back. Help us to be like you and treat others with love.

Amen.

Jesus Calls Disciples
Mark 1:16–20, Luke 5:27–29, John 1:35–50

When Jesus was an adult, he chose twelve men to stay with him to watch him teach, heal, pray, and do miracles. This week, we are going to learn the stories of how those men came to follow him!

Day 1. With your child (or using stuffed animals/dolls), act out the story found in Mark 1:16–20 of Jesus calling the fishermen. *SAY: What does a fisherman do? What kind of jobs do the people in our family do? Do you think Jesus wants us to follow him too, even though we're not fishermen? Yes, he does!*

Day 2. With your child (or using stuffed animals/dolls), act out the story found in Luke 5:27–29 of Jesus calling Levi. *SAY: Tax collectors were people who nobody liked, because they usually took extra money from people. Why do you think Jesus wanted to be friends with a tax collector? How can we show God's love to people who aren't very likeable?*

Day 3. Read John 1:43–50 as dramatically as possible. *SAY: Jesus showed Nathaniel a miracle—he knew what Nathaniel was doing even though he was far away. Can you do that? Do you think you would have followed Jesus if he told you something like that? Why, or why not?*

Day 4. Help your child draw a picture of Jesus and his twelve friends. *SAY: Why do you think Jesus wanted twelve friends? Who do you think Jesus wants to be his friend today?* (You, me, our family, others.)

Day 5. In Matthew 28:20, Jesus says, *"I am with you always..."* (NIV) It's a promise that Jesus made to his first disciples, and it's a promise he makes to us too, because he loves us. Help your child memorize the verse and remind them of Jesus' great love for his first friends, and for us!

PRAYER:

Dear Jesus, thank you for choosing twelve special friends when you were here on earth, and thank you for choosing me to be your friend forever too! Help me to show others what it means to be your friend forever.

Amen.

Jesus Loves Children

Mark 10:13–16

One day Jesus was standing around with a big crowd of people around him. Some parents brought their children to Jesus, hoping that he would pray for them. Jesus' friends thought he was *way* too important to talk to kids, so they told the kids to go away! But Jesus said, "Hey guys, I *love* kids! Let them come see me!" Then he put his hands on their heads and blessed the children.

Day 1. Act out the story using yourselves as actors, stuffed animals, or dolls. *ASK: Why do you think the kids wanted to see Jesus? If you had been there, would you have waited quietly in line to see Jesus or would you have jumped all over him and given him a hug? What would you have said to him?*

Day 2. *ASK: How old are you? Do you think Jesus loves you? How about after your next birthday… how old will you be then? Will Jesus still love you? How about after your next birthday? Will Jesus love me when I've had my next birthday? Does God love a baby who hasn't had any birthdays at all? God loves us no matter how many birthdays we've had!*

Day 3. Read Mark 10:13–16 out loud. *ASK: Who is the king in the kingdom of God? What do you think the kingdom of God is like? Would you like to be part of the Kingdom of God?*

Note: the kingdom of God refers to God's kingdom here on earth, not just heaven. Help your child imagine what would happen if love, joy, peace, patience, kindness, goodness, faithfulness, gentleness, and self-control were seen everywhere. What would this look like?

Day 4. Using a piece of paper, some scissors, and tape, make a crown with/for your child. Read Mark 10:11. *ASK: Did you know that you are a prince/princess in the kingdom of God? How does that make you feel?*

Day 5. *SAY: Just like Jesus blessed the children, I want to bless you too.* Take your child in your arms, put your hands on them, and bless them, saying, *"'The Lord bless you and keep you; the Lord make his face shine upon you and be gracious to you; the Lord turn his face toward you and give you peace.' In the name of Jesus, amen"* (Numbers 6:24–26, NIV). If you haven't already gotten into the habit of blessing your child, try doing this every night. You'll be surprised at how much your child will love being blessed, and how much you are blessed in return.

Wise for Salvation

PRAYER:

Thank you, Jesus, that you love me! I love you too.

Amen.

Jesus Cares for Us

Matthew 6:25–34

Jesus liked to tell people how much God loved them. One time he talked about how God takes care of the birds and flowers. Birds don't have to go to a grocery store or a restaurant to buy food, because God takes care of them and helps them find food in nature. And flowers don't have to go to the store to buy warm clothes in winter or pretty clothes for summer! God takes care of them and makes them beautiful. Just like God takes care of the birds and flowers, he wants us to know that he will care for us too.

Day 1. Pretend to be birds! Fly around, pecking seeds off the floor. Finish up by sitting down on a "branch" and tuck your heads under your "wings." *ASK: How does God take care of the birds? How does God take care of you and me?*

Day 2. Read the verses from the Matthew 6:25–34 while your child draws a picture of a flower or a bird. *SAY: What do you like most about this story that Jesus told?*

Wise for Salvation

Day 3. Have your child pretend to be a flower. Show them how to start as a tiny seed, then slowly grow as you give them water and sunshine. *SAY: Do you think this flower worries about how much water and sunshine it's going to get? Just like God provides these flowers with what they need to grow, God will provide you with what you need to grow. What do you need to grow?*

Day 4. If you have access to flowers outside, clip one and bring it to devotions with you. If not, just pretend to have one. Talk about what colour it is, how pretty it looks, and how God made it special and takes care of it.

Day 5. Practice the following verse while acting like a bird or flower: *"And my God will meet all your needs…"* (Philippians 4:19, NIV)

PRAYER:

Thank you, God, for taking care of the birds and flowers, and for taking care of us. Help us to trust you with our needs.

Amen.

Jesus Finds the Fish

Luke 5:1–11

One day Jesus was sitting in a boat near the shore, teaching people. When he was done, he asked Peter to move the boat and put his fishing nets in the water. Peter wasn't sure about this. He had already fished all night long and not found a single fish. He really needed to catch fish because fishing was his job, and he needed to sell some fish to feed his family. So he did as Jesus asked, and suddenly there were so many fish in the nets that the nets began to break! And when they pulled the fish into the boat, it started to sink because there were so many fish flopping around! Wow! Peter and his friends were very surprised, and they realized that Jesus can do anything.

Day 1. Review the story, then act it out with stuffed animals or yourselves as characters.

Day 2. Gather up a small blanket and several stuffed animals. Together with your child, hold the edges of the blanket so it looks like you are holding a fish net. At the beginning, the animals should be sitting on the floor. *SAY: Jesus' friends didn't know what was going to happen when they obeyed Jesus. But they did it anyway! Let's think of ways that we can obey Jesus, and each time we say something, we'll throw a "fish" into our "net" to remind us that God blesses us when we obey him!*

Wise for Salvation

Day 3. Sit on the edge of a bed or chair, and pretend to fish with a fishing pole together. *SAY: Let's pretend that we are fishing with Jesus. What would you like to say to Jesus while we're sitting here with him? What would Jesus want to say to you?*

Day 4. Read this story directly from the Bible (Luke 5:1–11) or from a children's Bible while your child draws a picture of a fish.

Day 5. *SAY: When Peter saw Jesus' miracle, he realized how many bad things he had done, and then he knelt in front of Jesus. Jesus forgave him and told him that they were going to work together from now on. Let's kneel down in front of Jesus right now and ask forgiveness for the bad things we have done.*

PRAYER:

Thank you, Jesus, for showing us your incredible power by filling up those nets with fish! Help us to trust you and to know that we can ask you for help with anything in our lives.

Amen.

Jesus Feeds the People

Mark 6:30–44

One day Jesus was with his friends, and many other people followed them and wanted to talk to Jesus. Jesus loved them, so he started teaching everyone. But it was getting late and the people were hungry. Jesus' friends thought it would be best to send the people home, but Jesus said to them, "*You* give them something to eat." His friends freaked out and went to find whatever food anyone would share. All they could find was five loaves of bread and two fish. Jesus told everyone to sit down, and then he prayed for the food. When they started passing it out, there kept being more and more food until over five thousand people had eaten! That's a lot of people to feed with only five loaves and two fish, but Jesus can do anything!

Day 1. Review the story, then act it out with stuffed animals or yourselves as characters. *ASK: What is your favourite part of this story?*

Day 2. *ASK: If you were really hungry, what would you like to eat? Would you eat bread and fish if you were super hungry? Who gives us the food we eat? God does! He helps us make money so that we can buy food from the grocery store, and he helps the farmers grow the food that we buy from the store. Let's thank God for feeding us!*

Wise for Salvation

Day 3. Count to the number five together, then to the number two. *SAY: That was how many loaves and fish the friends had to share. And how many people were there to feed? Five thousand! That's a lot of people. Could you share five loaves and two fish with that many people? No way! Only Jesus can do that. Let's thank Jesus for being so amazing.*

Day 4. Read this story directly from the Bible (Mark 6:30–44) or from a children's Bible while your child draws a picture of the bread and fish.

Day 5. *SAY: The Bible says that Jesus had "compassion" on the people, and that's why he taught them and fed them. Do you know what compassion is?* (Love for others that leads to helping them.) *Who is someone we can have compassion for? How can we help that person?*

PRAYER:

Thank you, Jesus, for being so loving and amazing that you would take a tiny little lunch and use it to feed so many people! Thank you for feeding us too.

Amen.

Jesus Walks on Water

Mark 6:45–51

After Jesus fed the five thousand people, he sent his disciples in a boat across the lake while he went up on a hill to pray. While the disciples were rowing the boat across the lake, a big wind started to blow. As the wind blew stronger, the waves grew bigger and it was very hard for them to row. In the middle of the night, Jesus started walking to them, and he walked right on top of the water in the middle of the windy waves! They were really scared, but Jesus said to them, "It's me! Don't be afraid." And when he got into the boat, the wind stopped right away. The friends were completely amazed!

Day 1. Review the story, then act it out with stuffed animals or yourselves as characters. *ASK: What is your favourite part of this story?*

Day 2. Put a little water in your bathtub or in a bucket. *ASK: If we stepped in this, would we sink or float? Do you think we can walk on the water? No way! Isn't Jesus amazing?*

Wise for Salvation

Day 3. Trace your child's foot on a piece of paper (preferably blue). Draw waves underneath it. *ASK: What does this have to do with the story we've been learning this week?* Put the picture up on a wall to remind you how powerful Jesus is!

Day 4. Read the story from the Bible (Mark 6:45–51) or from a children's Bible while your child draws a picture of wind and waves.

Day 5. *ASK: Do you know what I think about when I think about Jesus walking on the water? I know that he can walk on the water, that he can do anything. So when we need help, we can ask Jesus to help us. Can you think of anything that you (or someone else) needs help with?* Pray together, asking Jesus to help with the fear or struggle.

PRAYER:

Jesus, you are so amazing! I don't know anyone else who can walk on water. Thank you for showing us your incredible power and for helping us when we are afraid.

Amen.

Jesus Calms a Storm
Matthew 8:23–27

Jesus got into a boat with his friends and settled down to take a nap. Suddenly, a crazy storm blew over them and Jesus' friends were really scared! Strangely enough, Jesus kept snoozing right through the storm. The disciples woke him up and said, "Save us! We're going to drown!" Jesus stood up and told the wind and waves to be quiet… and they did! Everything became completely calm. Jesus' friends were totally amazed.

Day 1. Review the story, then act it out with stuffed animals or yourselves as characters. *ASK: What is your favourite part of this story?*

Day 2. *ASK: What does the Bible say Jesus was doing in the back of the boat? Can you sleep in a storm? Let's pretend that I'm sleeping, and you can try to wake me up by telling me that something big is going to happen.*

Wise for Salvation

Day 3. Pretend to be on a boat and make a storm by slapping your knees and making wind sounds. Together, make the noise and movement stop and start on command. *SAY: Can you believe that Jesus could just say one word and the storm would stop? I mean, imagine waves crashing, wind blowing, thunder and lightning booming, and rain pouring. Then all of the sudden, Jesus tells the storm to stop, and it does! Jesus had power over a storm!*

Day 4. Read this story directly from the Bible (Matthew 8:23–27) or from a children's Bible while your child draws a picture of a storm.

Day 5. *SAY: Do you know what I like to do when I'm scared? I like to think about how much Jesus loves me, that he wants to help me and that he is very, very strong. Remember, in our story we found out that Jesus was stronger than a huge storm. So whenever we are afraid, we can think about how much Jesus loves us, how strong he is, and how he takes care of us and we can pray and ask him to help us.*

Sometimes Jesus might not take the scary thing away. But he does promise that he will be with us and that he will help us as we deal with scary things. Jesus loves us very much. He wants to take care of us and help us grow stronger. Let's pray and ask Jesus to help us with some of these scary things. What scary thing would you like to pray about?

PRAYER:

Thank you, Jesus, that you take care of us. Even when it sometimes feels like you're asleep on the job, help us to see how you are working in our lives.

Amen.

Story of a Lost Sheep
Luke 15:3–7

Jesus told a lot of stories to the people who came to see him. He told the stories so that we could understand God better. One of the stories is about a shepherd who had one hundred sheep. That's a lot of sheep! But one day, one of the sheep went missing. Did the shepherd say, "Oh well, I still have lots of sheep"? No way! He went looking high and low for his little lost sheep. And when he found it, he carried it home on his shoulders. He was so excited that he told all his friends and neighbours about his sheep being found. That's how God feels about us. He will never leave you or stop being your friend.

Day 1. Read the paraphrase, then re-enact the story together using stuffed animals as your "flock." *ASK: Why do you think the shepherd went to go find his sheep?*

Day 2. Talk about a time when your child was lost, or lost something that was important to them. *ASK: How did you feel when you (or the object) were lost? Was it scary? How did you get found (or find your object)? It says right here in the Bible that if we are lost, God will look for us and keep looking for us until He finds us. The Bible tells us that we are so special to God.*

Day 3. Read the story directly from the Bible (Luke 15:3–7) or a children's Bible while your child draws a picture of a sheep.

Day 4. Hide a stuffed animal, then have your child go and look for it. Celebrate when it is found! Then remind your child of the following truth: "He will never leave you or stop being your friend" (Deuteronomy 31:8, paraphrase).

Day 5. *SAY: Let's think about all the places you could hide from me. Is there anywhere in this house you could hide where I wouldn't be able to find you? No, I would eventually find you wherever you were! In the same way, God always wants to be with you and he will go searching for you if you try to hide from him! How does that make you feel?*

PRAYER:

God, thank you for loving me so very much. Thank you that I am special to you and that you love me just as much as the shepherd in the story loved his sheep.

Amen.

Story of a Lost Son
Luke 15:11–19

Jesus told a lot of stories to the people who came to see him. He told the stories so that we could understand God better. One of the stories that Jesus told is about a boy who decided he didn't want to live with his family anymore, so he asked for a bunch of money from his dad and ran away from home! He was happy with his life for a while, but eventually his money ran out. The people he thought were his friends left him and he didn't know what to do. He took a job feeding pigs, and was so hungry that he wished he could eat pig food. Yuck. This part of the story shows us that sometimes we don't like being with God, and we run away. But running away from God is never a good idea!

Day 1. Read the paraphrase, then re-enact the story together.
ASK: Why do you think the son wanted to leave his family?

Day 2. Talk about a time when you disobeyed someone (like God or a parent), and then encourage your child to think of a time when he/she disobeyed. Remind him/her that God loves us even when we do wrong things.

Day 3. ASK: Do you think the boy's daddy was mad at him when he left? Do you think he said, "Go away, I never want to see you again." No? How do you think the daddy felt when the boy left? That's how God feels when we disobey him! But he still loves us.

Day 4. Read the story directly from the Bible (Luke 15:11–19) or from a children's Bible while your child draws a picture of the sad, hungry boy. (Be sure to stop reading before the son goes home. That's for another week!)

Day 5. SAY: Let's pretend that you are a pig and I am the lost boy who has to feed you. (Really ham it up here as you pretend to be the lost boy.) Oh, I'm SO hungry. I wish I could eat a bit of that pig food. It looks so gross, but just a little bit maybe? What's that? I'm not allowed to eat the pig food even? Oh no, but I'm SO hungry! Oh pig, what do you think I should do?

PRAYER:

Thank you, God, for loving me even when I make mistakes and do wrong things.

Amen.

Story of a Found Son
Luke 15:20–24

Jesus told a lot of stories to the people who came to see him. He told the stories so that we could understand God better. Remember that story about the boy who ran away from home? His life had gotten quite terrible so he decided to go home and apologize to his dad. He thought his dad would be really mad at him. But when he was still a long way away, his daddy saw him coming and he ran to his son and threw his arms around him! He gave him a big kiss, gave him some new clothes, and even a special ring. The dad was so excited that his son had returned home that he threw a giant party to show the world how happy he was.

Day 1. Read the paraphrase, then re-enact the story together.
ASK: Why do you think the son was scared to come home? Why wasn't the daddy angry?

Day 2. Have your child stand on the other side of the room and pretend to be hungry. Then have them run to you while you open your arms and say, "Welcome home!" Remind them that God will always love us, no matter what.

Day 3. Remind your child of the following truth: "He will never leave you or stop being your friend" (Deuteronomy 31:8, paraphrase). *ASK: How does the dad in this story act like God?*

Day 4. Read the story directly from the Bible (Luke 15:20–24) or from a children's Bible while your child draws a picture of their favourite part of a party (like some balloons or a cake).

Day 5. *ASK: What did the daddy in this story do to show his son that he loved him?* (Throw a party.) *What does God do to show you that he loves you?*

PRAYER:

Thank you, God, for loving me so much. Help us to remember your great love when we do wrong things, and to remember to say that we are sorry for the wrong things we've done.

Amen.

Story about a Big Party
Luke 14:16–24

Jesus told a lot of stories to the people who came to see him. He told the stories so that we could understand God better. One time Jesus told a story about a man who was going to have a great big party. He invited all his friends, but then they all decided that they didn't want to come. The man got really mad because he had set up this super amazing party and none of his friends wanted to come! He decided that he still wanted to have his great party, so he had his servant go and invite all the poor people, the sick people, the blind people, and the people who couldn't walk. They came and there was still more room, so the man told his servant to bring more and more people until the party was super full! This story was Jesus' way of telling us that he invites us all to be his friends.

Day 1. Read the paraphrase, then act out the story together. *ASK: What would you do if someone invited you to a big party?*

Day 2. *ASK: If you wanted to show your friends that you loved them, what would you do for them?* Try to do this thing this week, whether it is writing a letter, inviting a friend over, or baking some cookies!

Day 3. Remind your child of the following truth: "He will never leave you or stop being your friend" (Deuteronomy 31:8, paraphrase). *ASK: How does the man in this story act like God?*

Day 4. Read the story directly from the Bible (Luke 14:16–24) while your child draws a picture of their favourite party food.

Day 5. *ASK: If you were going to have a big party, what kind of people would you invite? What kind of people did the man invite? What kind of people does God invite to be his friend?*

PRAYER:

Dear God, thank you that we are all special to you, whether we are poor, sick, or just normal people. Help us to treat others the way you treat us!

Amen.

Jesus Heals a Blind Man

John 9:1–11

As Jesus went about his business, he saw a man who had been blind for his whole life. Jesus cared for the man and wanted to heal him. So he did something terribly gross: he spit into the dirt to make some mud, and then put it on the man's eyes! Then he told the man to go wash off the spit-mud. The man obeyed, and he was healed! For the first time in his life, he could see!

Day 1. Have your child draw a picture of mud while you read the story directly from the Bible (John 9:1–11). *ASK: What part of this story makes you happy? Does any of it make you sad?*

Day 2. Tie a piece of clothing or a blindfold over your child's eyes. Have your child try to walk around a bit. *ASK: How does that make you feel? Do you think you would like to live like that? How do you think the blind man felt when Jesus made him better?*

Day 3. Go into a room with no natural light and shut the door. *ASK: Are you scared? Would you be scared if you always had to be in the dark like the blind man did?* Come back into the light. Read Psalm 23:4: *"Even though I walk through the darkest valley, I will fear no evil, for you are with me; your rod and your staff, they comfort me"* (NIV). *SAY: We don't have to be afraid, because God is with us. The blind man learned that Jesus loved him very much, and Jesus loves us just as much!*

Day 4. You will need a piece of paper, tape, and a pair of scissors. Follow the directions below to make a simple paper lantern. Read Psalm 18:28: *"You, Lord, keep my lamp burning; my God turns my darkness into light"* (NIV). *SAY: When we are with God, we don't have to be afraid, because God can turn darkness into light, just like he turned the blind man's darkness into light. Let's keep this lantern close by to remind us that Jesus turns our darkness into light.*

Lantern directions: Fold an 8½ x 11 piece of paper in half to form a long, skinny rectangle. Use scissors to make ten to twelve vertical slits, starting at the fold. Don't cut all the way to the other end; leave about an inch at the top. Unfold the paper and turn it into a tube, with the slits vertical. Secure with tape.

Day 5. Together, think of at least five things that you are so happy that you can see. (Like rainbows, parents, etc.) Thank God for each of those items and the fact that you can see them.

PRAYER:

Thank you, God, for loving that blind man so much that you wanted to heal him. Thank you for being powerful enough to make him better. You are so amazing, and we love you!

Amen.

Jesus Heals a Lame Man
Mark 2:1–12

One day Jesus was teaching in a house, and there were so many people in the house that no one could get in or out! It was very squishy. But some people had a friend that they really wanted to get to Jesus. So they went up on the roof, *cut a hole*, and lowered the guy down on a mat! This man's legs didn't work, so he couldn't walk. Jesus cared for the man and wanted to heal him. So he told him to get up and walk, and just like that, the man was all better! Wow!

Day 1. Have your child draw a picture of the lame man's empty mat while reading the story from the Bible. *ASK: What part of this story makes you happy? Does any of it make you sad?*

Day 2. Try doing a couple of normal activities without legs. For example, if it's bedtime, get changed without standing, or if it's mealtime, try to go wash hands without using your legs. *SAY: Our legs are pretty important! What do you think the lame man did all day when he couldn't use his legs? How do you think he felt when Jesus healed him?*

Day 3. Think of one family member or friend who deals with knee problems or other foot/leg problems (bunions, arthritis, etc.). *ASK: Do you think that God could make their legs better? He sure could. Do you think we should ask him right now?* Pray together, asking that God would provide relief and even heal their legs entirely.

Day 4. *SAY: The Bible says that amazing things will happen when God comes to save his people.* Read Isaiah 35:6: *"Then will the lame leap like a deer, and the mute tongue shout for joy. Water will gush forth in the wilderness and streams in the desert"* (NIV). *SAY: Those amazing things are called "miracles," and they are things that only God can do. What other things would be a miracle?* Thank God for how amazing and powerful he is.

Day 5. Together, think of at least five things that you like to do with your legs. Do them, if possible, then thank God for each of those activities and the fact that you can do them.

PRAYER:

Thank you, God, for loving that lame man so much that you wanted to heal him. Thank you for being powerful enough to make him better. You are so amazing, and we love you!

Amen.

Jesus Heals Ten Lepers
Luke 17:11–19

One day Jesus was walking in the country, and 10 ten men called out to him, "Jesus! Have pity on us!" They wanted Jesus to heal them, because their sickness was so terrible that no one would touch them anymore. No hugs from their moms, no high-fives from their friends, not even a touch on the head. These men hoped so much that Jesus would decide to heal them. And you know what? Jesus loved these men *so* much, and he knew that no one else had loved them in a long time. So he healed them! He just said to them, "Go! Show the others that you are healed!" They did, and they were healed.

Day 1. Have your child draw a picture of a sick person's face while you read the story from the Bible. *ASK: What part of this story makes you happy? Does any of it make you sad?*

Day 2. With your child, act out a sickness—coughing, throwing up, having no voice, itching… whatever you can think of. *ASK: What do you think it would be like to be sick all the time? Would you enjoy that? Leprosy was a terrible disease and you could never get better from it. How do you think the lepers felt when Jesus healed them?*

Day 3. Read another story of Jesus healing a leper (Mark 1:40–42). *SAY: It says that Jesus was filled with compassion. What is compassion?* (Loving someone so much that you want to help them.) Pray that your family would be like Jesus—full of compassion.

Day 4. Read Luke 17:15–19. *ASK: Why do you think only one guy came back to say thank you? Do you think Jesus likes it when we say thank you? Let's think of five things that we love, that we can thank God for right now.*

Day 5. Think of one family member or friend who is sick. *ASK: Do you think that God could make them better? He sure could. Do you think we should ask him right now?* Pray together, asking that God would provide relief and even heal them entirely.

PRAYER:

Thank you, God for loving those sick men so much and for healing all of them. Help us to be thankful for all you've done for us. We love you!

Amen.

Jesus Raises Lazarus

John 11:1–44

This week we'll be going through the whole story bit by bit. This story will probably open up a lot of questions about life, death, and heaven with your child. I encourage you to be honest with them, answering questions truthfully and biblically. When you don't know the answer, seek it out together by bringing your questions to the Lord and asking him to help you understand.

Day 1. Read John 11:1, 4–6. *ASK: What would you do if you were Jesus and your friend was sick? Do you know any sick people?*

Day 2. Read John 11:17. *SAY: This means that by the time Jesus got all the way over to his friend's house, his friend Lazarus had died, and they had buried him four days ago. How would you feel if someone you knew died and you would never see them again?* Read John 1:32–36. *ASK: How did Jesus feel when he found out about Lazarus' death? How do you think he feels when other people in the world die?*

Day 3. Draw a picture of the story while reading John 11:38–44. *ASK: How does this part of the story make you feel? Why do you think Jesus made Lazarus alive again?* (A clue is in verse 42.)

Day 4. Read John 11:23–26. *SAY: Here Jesus is telling us that when we believe in him, we will live forever with him in heaven. What do you know about heaven?* Allow your child to dream a bit about what heaven will be like. A good resource to look up if your child has a lot of questions is a book called *Someday Heaven* by Larry Libby.[2] It is a beautiful book that gives a lot of insight into the topic. *SAY: Jesus asks Martha if she believes him—do you believe what Jesus says in these verses?*

Day 5. Act out the last part of the story with your child (John 11:38–44). *ASK: What is your favourite part of the story? Did you know that Jesus loves you just as much as Jesus loved Lazarus and his sisters? How does that make you feel?*

PRAYER:

Thank you, God, for showing everyone how amazing you are. Thank you that you loved Mary and Martha and Lazarus, and that you are powerful enough to heal him, even after he died.

Amen.

---

2 Larry Libby, *Someday Heaven* (Grand Rapids, MI: Zondervan, 2010).

Woman at the Well
John 4:1–29, 39–42

One day Jesus was walking through Samaria, which was a place that Jewish people didn't like to go. They considered the Samaritans their enemies. But Jesus stopped at a well to talk to a lady who had no friends. He told her that he loved everyone and had come to give them eternal life. She was so excited that she told everyone in her town about Jesus' great love!

Day 1. Act out the story with your child. *ASK: Why do you think Jesus stopped to talk with the lady? What did he ask for? What do you think he really wanted?*

Day 2. Have your child draw a picture of a bucket of water while you read the story straight from the Bible (John 4:4–14). *ASK: What's your favourite part of the story? Why?*

Day 3. Read John 4:9. *SAY: Jesus loves everyone. Jesus even loves people who others may not like a whole lot—like the Samaritans. Have you ever had a hard time getting along with someone? Do you think Jesus wants you to love people, even when you don't play together well? Let's pray that you would show Jesus' love.*

Christie Thomas

Day 4. Read John 4:28–30, 39–42. *SAY: Because Jesus stopped and showed love to one lonely lady, a whole town full of people came to believe that he is the Saviour of the world. Let's think of one lonely person who we could show love to this week.* (Write down the name and how you're going to show love.) *Perhaps by showing Jesus' love to him/her, another whole town full of people will come to believe in Jesus!*

Day 5. Get a cup of water, then read John 4:10–15. *SAY: If we drink this cup of water now, will we be able to go through the rest of our lives without drinking? What about if we drink a glass of milk? No matter what we drink, we will always need more drinks to keep us alive. Jesus is talking about giving us something that will fill up our souls so we never want for anything more—because we are filled with Jesus' love.*

PRAYER:

Dear Jesus, thank you for showing love to the woman at the well. Teach us to show love to those who we think are unlovable.

Amen.

Zacchaeus

Luke 19:1–10

Zacchaeus was a very small man with a very small heart. He took money from people through taxes and kept a lot of it for himself. But when Jesus came through town, Zacchaeus climbed a tree in order to see him. And when Jesus came by the tree, he asked Zacchaeus to come down and invited himself over! When he learned about Jesus' love, Zacchaeus' heart grew to love God and people.

Day 1. Measure how tall your child is against a doorjamb or a wall. *SAY: How tall do you think Zacchaeus was? No matter how tall we are, Jesus loves us. He loves you when you're this tall, and he'll love you when you're taller than me! How big do you think your heart is? No matter how much love you have, Jesus loves you more!*

Day 2. Read the story from a children's Bible or from Luke 19:1–10 while your child draws a picture of a tree. *SAY: What is your favourite part of this story? Why?*

Day 3. Act out the story with your child. *SAY: Did you learn something new from the story today? What was it?*

Day 4. Pretend to go for a walk with your child. Suddenly, stop and look up as if you are looking at Zacchaeus in the tree. *ASK: Would you have stopped to talk to the guy nobody else liked? Why do you think Jesus looked up and talked to Zacchaeus when he was in the tree?*

Day 5. Read Luke 19:8. *SAY: What did Zacchaeus do?* Together with your child, pray and listen for God's ideas on how you could respond to God's love. It might be something like giving some of your possessions to the poor, or it might be something else. Ask God to give you and your child creativity, be open to his response, and then obey!

PRAYER:

Dear Jesus, thank you for showing your deep, deep love to Zacchaeus and for reminding us that you love us, no matter how big we are or who we are. Help us to love like you.

Amen.

Jesus' Death, Resurrection, and Ascension

There are two schools of thought on whether or not preschoolers are ready to hear the Easter story. Some children's ministries teach the Last Supper, then skip right to the resurrection because they believe the crucifixion is too disconcerting for preschoolers.

As it is the central tenet of our faith, I believe they need to hear it. In a culture where it is normal for a preschooler to watch movies about superheroes (where there is a decent amount of death and destruction), I think it is quite appropriate for them to talk about the death of Christ.

They won't understand the full significance of his death and the sadness it brought his followers, but that's no reason to avoid teaching about Jesus' sacrifice for us. Let them hear it, let them be moved by the sadness of his friends, and let them rejoice all the more in the resurrection because they have seen the alternative!

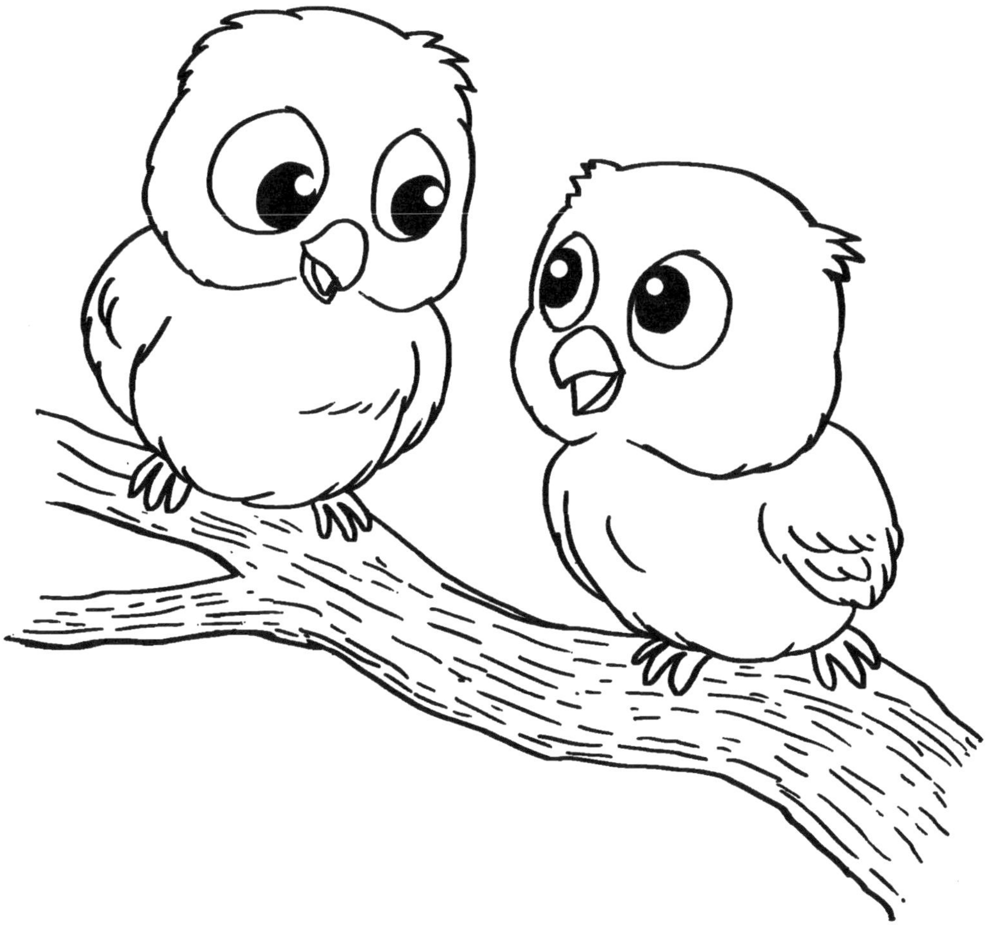

Palm Sunday

Matthew 21:1–9

Jesus came with his friends to Jerusalem, and before they went into town, he sent two of his friends to get a donkey. When they brought the donkey back, they put their coats on top and Jesus sat on them! This is how he rode into Jerusalem, the most important city around. A very large crowd came into town and put their coats on the road. They also got tree branches and put them on the road for the donkey and Jesus to ride on. Then they shouted, "Hosanna in the highest! Blessed is he who comes in the name of the Lord!"

Day 1. Act out the story using yourselves, stuffed animals, or dolls. *ASK: Why do you think the people got so excited? What is your favourite part of this story? Why?*

Day 2. *ASK: If Jesus walked into this room right now, what words would you say to him?* (Wait for answers.) *The people in the story shouted "Hosanna!" which means "Hooray! We are saved!" Let's practice shouting "Hosanna" to Jesus right now!*

Day 3. *ASK: If you were a king or queen coming into a city, how would you like to come into town? Would you ride a donkey or would you come on something fancier?*

For those aged five or older: *Did you know that a man named Zechariah knew that Jesus was going to ride into Jerusalem on a donkey (instead of a horse or a chariot) way before Jesus was even born?* Read Zechariah 9:9. *How do you think Zechariah knew this would happen?* (God told him.) *That verse was a clue to the people in Jesus' time that he was going to be the king of the whole world. Do you think that Jesus is a good king?*

Day 4. Read Matthew 21:15–16. *SAY: When the leaders heard the kids praising Jesus in the temple, Jesus told them that God loves it when kids sing praise to him. Let's sing a song of praise to God right now, because we know that he will love it!* Sing one of your child's favourite songs about Jesus. If you can't think of any praise songs your child knows, sing "Jesus Loves Me."

Day 5. Use a piece of paper and crayons to trace your child's hands. Help them cut the hands out. Wave the paper hands like palm branches. Have your child repeat the words of the people's praises after you: "Hosanna to the Son of David! Blessed is he who comes in the name of the Lord! Hosanna in the highest! Hosanna!"

PRAYER:

Thank you, Jesus, for loving us and coming to earth to be the king of our hearts. Help us to always love you and be excited by you, just like the people in this story were excited to see you.

Amen.

Easter: The Short Edition (Ages 2–3)
Matthew 26–28

There were some bad guys who didn't like Jesus, so they decided that they would try to get him in trouble. They arrested him and got everyone to be mad at him, then sent him to die on a cross! Even though Jesus hadn't done anything wrong, he still took the punishment. After he died, his friends rolled up his body in some sheets and laid him in cave, with a big rock over the door. Three days later, some of his friends came by to put perfume on his body, except that it wasn't there! Instead, an angel stood by the cave and told them that Jesus was alive! They were so surprised, but also very excited so they ran off to tell all their other friends the good news.

Day 1. Read the paraphrase, then act it out with your child.

Note: This story can be quite horrifying to an imaginative or empathetic child. If your child has questions, answer them as best you can, and share with them your own feelings about Jesus' death. If you're fairly matter-of-fact about it, your child will be as well.

Day 2. ASK: How do you think his friends felt after he died? Why? Would you have felt that way?

Wise for Salvation

Day 3. Read the story from a simple children's Bible while your child draws a picture of a cross.

Day 4. Together, try to push a wall as if you are pushing the rock away from Jesus' tomb. *SAY: This is what it would be like for just one person to try to move the rock in front of the cave. How do you think the angel did it?*

Day 5. *ASK: Let's use our imaginations… what do you think Jesus did when he first came back to life? Where did he go? What was the first word he said?*

PRAYER:

Thank you, Jesus, for dying and coming back to life. You are really amazing! Help us to understand what this means for our lives.

Amen.

Easter: The Extended Edition (Ages 4+)

Matthew 26–28

Note: We will be slowly going through the Easter story, with ten installments over two weeks.

I highly recommend reading each section of the Easter story from a children's Bible. *The Jesus Storybook Bible*, by Sally Lloyd-Jones,[3] is fantastic, and I have set up each day's reading based on the sections presented in her book. If you don't have access to her book, I have indicated the verses that go along with each part of the story.

Day 1. Jesus washes his friends' feet. Read John 13:3–9, 14–15 (pages 286–288 in JSB).

Now, do as Jesus commands and wash your child's feet—in a tub, a sink, or just with wet cloths. Allow your child to wash your feet as well. *SAY: How did you feel when you washed my feet? How does it make you feel that Jesus would wash our dirty feet? Why do you think Jesus wants us to do this?*

Day 2. The Last Supper. Read Mark 14:22–24 (pages 291–292 in JSB). *SAY: Did you know that Jesus came to rescue us? Do you know why we need to be rescued? We need rescuing because we do bad things, called sin, and those bad things keep us from God. Jesus wants to rescue us from our sin—to forgive us and to help us change. Think of one or two things today for which you need forgiveness and ask Jesus to rescue you from that sin.*

---

3   *The Jesus Storybook Bible*, Sally Lloyd-Jones (Grand Rapids, MI: Zondervan, 2012).

Wise for Salvation

Day 3. Jesus prays in the garden. Read Mark 14:32–42 (pages 294–296 in JSB). *SAY: Jesus was very sad, because he knew that all of our badness was going to go into his heart. How does it make you feel that all the badness in your heart had to go into Jesus' heart? That because of the bad things you and I have done, Jesus had to be punished? Do you think that's fair? I don't think that's fair. But because Jesus loves us so much, that's what he chose to do. Let's thank him right now for being so wonderful to us!*

Day 4. Jesus is arrested. Read Mark 14:43–50 (pages 299–300 in JSB). *SAY: Why did Peter slice off the man's ear?* (Because he was afraid, and he was trying to protect Jesus.) *What would you have done if someone came to arrest your best friend? Even though Jesus could have stopped them from arresting him, he didn't. Why not?*

Day 5. Jesus' trial. Read Mark 14:53–64 (page 301 in JSB). *SAY: Do you think Jesus was afraid to die? Can you think of a reason why the leaders would hate Jesus so much?* (They were afraid of him and the Romans, they didn't like people who were different, they were jealous…) *It's a terrible thing that these leaders hated Jesus. Yet God used them in his great rescue plan. Jesus had to die, and he used these mean and jealous leaders to make his plan work. But Jesus didn't hate the leaders back. He wants us to love people who hurt us. Let's pray that we would be able to love those who make us feel bad.*

Day 6. Jesus is crucified. Read Mark 15:25–34 (pages 302–304 in JSB). *SAY: Do you know why Jesus stayed on that cross? It was love. Who does Jesus love? He loves YOU. _____ (name), Jesus loves YOU so much that he chose to take the punishment for the wrong things YOU'VE done. How does that make you feel? Would you like to say something to Jesus?*

Day 7. Jesus dies and is buried. Read Mark 15:37–46 (pages 306–308 in JSB). *SAY: How do you think Jesus' friends felt as they buried his body in the tomb? How would you feel if your best friend died? I think they were probably terribly sad. But did you know that the story doesn't end here? Jesus had to die to take the punishment for our sin, but he also had another thing he had to do!*

Day 8. Jesus' body is gone. Read Mark 16:1–8 (pages 310–312 in JSB).

SAY: Wow, wasn't that a surprise?! How would you feel if you saw a huge, shiny angel? What did you think of the angel's news? Do you think you would have believed him if you had been one of those women?

Wise for Salvation

Day 9. Jesus talks to Mary. Read John 20:11–18 (pages 314–317 in JSB). *SAY: What sad things had God made better? Mary was so excited to see Jesus, because she had thought he was going to be dead forever. But Jesus is God's Son and he couldn't stay dead—he had to come back to life so that death could come untrue, so that all the people who love him can eventually came back to life too. Do you or I know anyone who has died that someday will come back to life? How do you think we will feel when we see them? Will we feel like Mary did—excited and joyful and a little bit scared?*

Day 10. Jesus appears to his friends. Read Luke 24:36–43 (pages 318–321 in JSB). *SAY: Touch me. Am I real? Jesus' friends thought he wasn't really there, but when they touched him, they felt that he was just as real as you or me. But the Bible tells us that Jesus' body was not only real, it was better than real—it could never get sick or hurt or die ever again. The great news is that someday Jesus will give us bodies just like that too! How do you feel about that? Let's thank God for his amazing rescue plan!*

Road to Emmaus

Luke 24:13–32

Two of Jesus' friends were walking to a town when they came upon another man who started walking with them. They told this man all about what had happened with Jesus—that he was so wonderful, but that bad people had put him on a cross to die, and that some of Jesus' friends were saying that he was alive again. The stranger started explaining lots of things to them, and telling them why it was important for Jesus to die and come back to life. These two men then invited the stranger for supper. When he was at the table with them, he took bread, gave thanks, broke the bread, and began to give it to them. Then they suddenly realized that the man was actually *Jesus!* But just as soon as they figured it out, Jesus disappeared! They were so surprised, because now they knew for sure that Jesus was alive again, and they went to tell all their friends.

Day 1. Read the paraphrase, then act it out with your child or using stuffed animals.

Day 2. ASK: Why do you think the two men didn't recognize Jesus right away? How would you recognize Jesus? What do you think he looks like?

Wise for Salvation

Day 3. Have your child draw a picture of three people as you read the story from the Bible (Luke 24:13–32) or from a children's Bible.

Day 4. *ASK: What did Jesus' friends do when they recognized him?* (Hint: see verses 33–35). *Let's try running around and telling everyone the great news!* (Jesus is alive!)

Day 5. You will need a piece of paper and a crayon/pencil. Trace your child's footprint and write the following verse inside the print: *"I have called you friends..."* (John 15:15, NIV). Practice saying it together.

PRAYER:

Jesus, that was a pretty neat thing you did when you showed up to explain all about your death to your friends and then let them see who you really were later. Please help us to recognize your presence in our lives.

Amen.

The Great Commission

Matthew 28:16–20

After he came back to life, Jesus told his friends to meet him on a mountain. Jesus met them there and told them that they had a new job to do! Their job was to tell everyone they met about Jesus' love, teaching them about God the Father, God's Son Jesus, and the Holy Spirit. They were to teach everyone how to follow and love Jesus. And Jesus promised to be with them always, even if they couldn't see him.

Day 1. Read and act out the story. *ASK: What do you think about Jesus' instructions?*

Day 2. You will need a map (physical or digital) or a globe. Show your child some of the parts of the earth and talk about how God loves everyone in the whole world and wants them to love him too.

Day 3. *SAY: Jesus gave his friends a special message to tell the world. Do you remember what that special message is?* (Use "Jesus wants to be your friend forever" or some variant of that message.) *Let's practice telling each other that special message.*

Wise for Salvation

Day 4. *SAY: There are many different ways that we can tell people about Jesus' love. We can send emails or letters, tell people on the phone, or just shout it out loud! Let's pick one way and try it out today.*

Day 5. Read the story from the Bible (Matthew 28:16–20) while your child draws a picture of the earth.

PRAYER:

Thank you, Jesus, for loving us! Help us to share your love with everyone we meet.

Amen.

Jesus Goes to Heaven

John 14:1–4 and Acts 1:6–11

After his resurrection, Jesus' friends were still expecting him to kick out the bad king and sit on his throne. But instead, he told them that *they* were going to be making disciples now. He also said that he would send a special helper to help them. This would be the Holy Spirit. Then, as Jesus' friends stood watching from a hillside, Jesus went back up into heaven. Up, up, up he went as his friends stretched their necks to see where he was going. Where was he going? Two angels came to talk to the confused friends and told them that Jesus was going to prepare a place for them, and for us! One day, he will return to earth to be our King.

Day 1. Act out the story with your child. If you have access to dolls or stuffed animals, use them as all the other people watching Jesus go, and/or as the angels.

Day 2. Read Acts 1:6–11 while your child draws a picture of the sky. *ASK: Where did Jesus go? Why did he go? How do you think his friends felt as they watched him go up into the sky?*

Wise for Salvation

Day 3. Read John 14:1–4. *ASK: How many rooms are in our home?* (If you are able, go through and count your rooms and talk about the purpose of each room.) *Jesus said that he was going to prepare a place in his house with many rooms. How big do you think Jesus' house is? What do you think Jesus' house is like? What do you think will be the best part of Jesus' house?*

Day 4. *ASK: What part of this story makes you happy? Sad? Mad? Jesus said he would never leave them, but he went up to heaven. So what do you think it means that he will never leave us?*

Day 5. Help your child memorize the following verse, and give them a big high-five when they can say it alone! *"Go and make disciples of all nations…"* (Matthew 28:19, NIV). *SAY: When Jesus went up to heaven, he gave all of his friends, including us, a special job—we are supposed to "make disciples," which means that we need to tell people about Jesus! Today let's pray that God will give us courage to tell others about Jesus' love.*

PRAYER:

Dear Jesus, thank you for going up to heaven to prepare a special place for us! You love us so much and we love you too. Help us to do the job that you asked us to do–to go everywhere and tell everyone the happy news about your love.

Amen.

The Early Church

In Old Testament times, the Holy Spirit came upon people who had a special task, like Moses and the judges. In 1 Samuel 16:13, Samuel anointed David as the future king, and as he did this, *"from that day on the Spirit of the Lord came upon David in power"* (NIV).

But it turns out that the Holy Spirit isn't just for the leaders of Israel. Just before Jesus ascended to heaven, he commanded his disciples not to leave Jerusalem,

> But wait for the gift my Father promised, which you have heard me speak about. For John baptized with water, but in a few days you will be baptized with the Holy Spirit. (Acts 1:4-5, NIV)

God the Son, a human being who could only be in one place at one time, left so that all God's people could be filled with God the Spirit, just like Moses and David had been. The Bible shows us that the Holy Spirit is a Person of God, and his role is to help every disciple become more like Jesus and share the gospel.

After the disciples were filled with the Holy Spirit at Pentecost, Peter preached to all the Jews who had come into Jerusalem for the holy days. He told them,

> Repent and be baptized, every one of you, in the name of Jesus Christ for the forgiveness of your sins. And you will receive the gift of the Holy Spirit. The promise is for you <u>and your children and for all who are far off—for all</u> whom the Lord our God will call. (Acts 2:38-39, NIV, emphasis added)

So who is this Holy Spirit? He is one of the Trinity, the three Persons of God: God the Father, God the Son, and God the Holy Spirit. All three are present throughout Scripture, and all three are fully God. Yet there are not three gods to worship, but one God: *"Here, O Israel: The Lord our God, the Lord is one"* (Deuteronomy 6:4, NIV). Just like in that old hymn, the One we worship is "God in three persons, blessed Trinity!"

This is one of the most complex ideas in all theology, and as adults, our heads hurt when we think about it too long. Yet the early years are the perfect time to introduce the concept. Preschool children usually fully accept the possibility of three-in-one, because they truly have childlike faith. Questions will come as they get older, but in the meantime they'll have a few years to accept this fact without wondering about its intricacies.

One premise upon which I base all of my spiritual interactions with children is that the Holy Spirit in them is the same Holy Spirit that is in an adult. He is not a smaller Holy Spirit just because the vessel is smaller. Never underestimate the power of the Holy Spirit that can be manifested in the smallest child! Children have started charities, brought about physical healing, and loved the unlovable in the power of the Holy Spirit.

Pentecost

Acts 2:1–6

After Jesus went up to heaven, his friends gathered all together. One day, the house they were in suddenly got really windy inside, even with no windows open! As the people looked around, they saw something that looked like fire on each person's head. This was the Holy Spirit. He was coming to fill them up with God's power and give them courage to tell others about God's love. As soon as this happened, they all ran outside and starting telling everyone about Jesus. There were people from many different countries in the city at that time, and Jesus' friends found themselves suddenly able to speak in each of the different languages, so that every person in the crowd could hear about Jesus.

Day 1. Read the paraphrase together, then act out the story with your child. *SAY: Pentecost is the birthday of the Church, because it's when Jesus' friends received the Holy Spirit and started telling the whole world about His death and resurrection. That was over two thousand years ago and now there are millions of people all over the world who love Jesus. Together, we are called the Church. Let's sing Happy Birthday to the Church as a way to celebrate!* If you know how to sing "Happy Birthday" in another language, this would be a good time to teach your kids.

Day 2. Read the story out of Acts 2:1–6. *ASK: What kind of languages can you speak? Try a few words in another language, like French or Spanish. What did Jesus' friends do when they discovered they could speak other languages?* (The answer is found in Acts 2:11.)

One of the gifts that the Holy Spirit gives is the ability to tell other people about Jesus in a language that we haven't learned. Let's pray for people in other parts of the world that someone would come to them and teach them about Jesus in their own language.

Day 3. Read Acts 2:2. *ASK: What do you think a "violent wind" would sound like?* Try blowing as hard as you can to make a sound that can fill your whole house. *ASK: Where do you think the wind came from?*

Day 4. Pretend to light a fire together (or you can light a real candle). Talk about how it would feel to have your body covered in fire. Would it be hot? See if you can think of another story in the Bible where there was a fire that didn't burn anything up. (Hint, look in Exodus!) That was also God's Spirit!

Wise for Salvation

Day 5. Draw a flame on a piece of paper and tape it to your child's back to remind them that anyone who is a child of God is filled with the Holy Spirit, just like the disciples. It just might not be quite as outwardly obvious as having a flame of fire on your head!

PRAYER:

God, thank you so much for sending the gift of the Holy Spirit to the disciples and to me. Help me to love you more and more each day.

Amen.

Timothy Learns the Scriptures

2 Timothy 1:5, 3:14–15

Timothy was a boy who learned all about Jesus and the Bible from his mother and grandmother. When he got a little older, he worked with a man named Paul. Together, Timothy and Paul explored much of the world, teaching everyone they met about Jesus. Because Timothy was taught about the Bible when he was very young, he was able to become a leader in the church when he was still a young man!

Day 1. Act out how you think Timothy would have learned from his mother and grandmother when he was a boy. Did they read him books? Tell him stories? Bring him to church? *SAY: What do you think are the most important things that his mother taught him? What are the most important things your mother teaches you?*

Day 2. Read 2 Timothy 1:5 and 3:14–15 aloud while your child draws a picture of a Bible. *SAY: This verse means that Timothy knew God's word even when he was a very little boy. Do you know God's stories and his love?*

Day 3. Read 1 Timothy 4:12. *SAY: This verse means that even though you are young, you can follow God just like an adult can. You can be the one to remind adults about faith and love! What are some things you can do to be a good example for others?*

Wise for Salvation

Day 4. Read 1 Timothy 6:18. *SAY: This is another thing that Timothy learned. What does this mean to you? How can you be like this verse says this week? Remember that we cannot do these things alone—we need to ask the Holy Spirit to help us!*

Day 5. Read 2 Timothy 1:14. The following truth has been taken from this verse: "The Holy Spirit lives in us and will help us." Practice it together with your child!

PRAYER:

God, thank you for all the people who teach us about you. Help me to learn about you and love you more each day!

Amen.

Peter and John Go to the Temple

Acts 3:1–11

Peter and John went to the temple together one day, and they met a man who sat in front of the gates every day. This man was crippled, which means that he couldn't walk. He asked Peter and John for some money. Peter and John looked at the man and decided they wouldn't give him any money this time, but they would give him something much better. Peter told him to get up and walk! The Holy Spirit gave Peter the power to heal, just like Jesus did when he lived on Earth! The man jumped right up and began to walk. He went with them and started running and jumping and praising God. Everyone who saw him was amazed.

Day 1. Act out the story with your child, using stuffed animals or dolls as extra characters if available. *ASK: What is your favourite part of this story? Why?*

Day 2. Read the story out of the Bible (Acts 3:1–11) while your child draws a picture of a guy sitting. *SAY: Did you learn anything new in the story today?*

Wise for Salvation

Day 3. *ASK: Do you remember another story like this in the Bible?* (Check out Mark 2:1–4, 12. *ASK: Who did the first miracle of healing a crippled man?* (Jesus.) *Why do you think Peter and John were also able to heal a crippled man?* (They did it in the name of Jesus Christ; they were empowered by the Holy Spirit, who had just come to be with them; and they had the Spirit of God giving them power, so they were able to do a lot of miracles like Jesus did!)

Day 4. Pretend that you are the crippled man. Try to do some normal activities without using your legs. How does it feel? Then say, "In the name of Jesus Christ, walk!" And jump up! Do all kinds of things with your legs—jumping, walking, dancing, karate kicks—whatever fills you and your child with joy.

Day 5. Read John 14:12. *SAY: What kind of works did Jesus do?* (Healing, loving, feeding many people, bringing people back to life.) *Jesus said that anyone who believes in him will be able to do even greater things than he did! That's because we have the Holy Spirit filling us with courage and power.*

PRAYER:

God, thank you for the amazing miracles that Jesus' friends were able to do because your Spirit filled them with the power of God. Help me to trust in your Spirit to help me do things that seem impossible!

Amen.

Tabitha Is Healed
Acts 9:36–42

There was a lady named Tabitha who helped a lot of people, and she was very much loved. She would sew beautiful clothes for people who were poor. But then she got sick and died. Her friends were very sad, so they called Peter and asked him to bring her back to life. He walked into the room where her body was, and prayed. Then he said, "Tabitha, get up." She came back to life, opened her eyes, and popped up! Because of Peter's amazing miracles, many people believed in Jesus.

Day 1. Act out this story with your child. As you do, talk about the different emotions the people in the story might have experienced, such as love, sadness, fear, courage, and joy.

Day 2. Read the story right out of Acts 9:36–42 while your child draws a picture of a piece of clothing. *SAY: What is your favourite part of this story?*

Day 3. *SAY: There are two people in this story whom the Holy Spirit helped to do wonderful things. Who are they?* (Peter and Tabitha.) *What special job did the Holy Spirit help Tabitha do?* (See verses 36 and 39 for answers.) *Let's ask the Holy Spirit to help us know what our special jobs are, and to help us do them.*

Day 4. Pick out a few pieces from your child's wardrobe, and find out where they are made. *SAY: Tabitha was a person who helped poor people by sewing clothes for them. Today, the people who sew our clothes are usually poor because they don't get paid very much. See these tags? These clothes were made in _____ (Bangladesh, India, Thailand, etc). We need to pray for these people that someone like Tabitha would help them in their need. We also need to pray that the Holy Spirit would show us how we can help.* Spend time praying together.

Day 5. Read Acts 9:40. *SAY: What did Peter do before he was able to bring Tabitha back to life? We need to learn to talk to God about everything and to listen to him back. As we learn to do that better, we may be able to do amazing miracles through the Holy Spirit just like Peter. Let's talk to God right now.*

PRAYER:

Thank you, God, for doing something so amazing and bringing Tabitha back to life. Help me to be like Peter, who through your power brought Tabitha back to life. And help me to be like Tabitha, who was always helping people in need.

Amen.

Peter Gets out of Jail Free
Acts 12:3–17

The king of Israel didn't like Peter and his friends very much because he was afraid of God's mighty power working in them. So the king arrested Peter and put him in jail. One night, while his friends prayed for him, an angel came to Peter and helped him escape from jail. Peter went to the house where his friends were and they were so surprised to see him that they almost forgot to let him in the door! In the morning, no one at the jail could figure out where Peter had gone, because God had set him free!

Day 1. Act out the story with your child or colour the picture together. *ASK: What do you find most surprising about this story?*

Day 2. Read the story out of Acts 12:3–10 while your child draws a picture of a jail. *ASK: Why do you think Peter thought the angel wasn't real, that he was just dreaming? Have you ever seen an angel or something that others might think was just a dream?*

Day 3. Play a short game of "Follow the Leader" with your child while pretending that one of you is Peter in jail and one of you is the angel who says, "Follow me." *ASK: What would you think if an angel came to you and said to follow him?*

Christie Thomas

Day 4. Read Acts 12:11–17, then act out or talk about this part of the story together. *ASK: Why do you think the people were so surprised to see Peter?*

Day 5. If you are able, spend a couple minutes on the computer before doing this devotion. Go to www.persecution.net and look at the "Persecution and Prayer Alert" for news about persecution of Christians in other countries. Find one that you feel is appropriate for your child, and use it to pray specifically. *SAY: The Bible doesn't say that Peter was freed from prison just because the church prayed for him, but it does say that God listens to our prayers. There are many pastors and Christians who are in jail in other countries right now. Let's pray for people in _____ (country) who are being hurt and put in jail by people who don't understand God's love.*

PRAYER:

Thank you, God, for setting Peter free from jail so he could continue to teach others about you! Help us to remember that you really do answer prayers, even when they seem impossible.

Amen.

Paul Escapes from Damascus
Acts 9:19–25

Saul (who we later call Paul) was a bad man, but Jesus changed his heart and he started to tell everyone around how amazing Jesus is. Some people didn't like that, so they made a plan to hurt him. His friends found out about the plan to hurt Saul, and they snuck him out of the city by putting him in a basket and lowering him down from the city wall in the middle of the night!

Day 1. Review the story with your child, either by acting it out together or telling it in a dramatic voice. *ASK: What's your favourite part of this story?*

Day 2. Have your child draw a picture of a basket while reading the story straight from the Bible. *ASK: Why do you think those people wanted to hurt Saul?*

Day 3. Have your child sit in a laundry basket while you either wiggle it around or pick it up and carry it around. *ASK: How do you think Saul felt when they were lowering him in a basket through an opening in the wall? Do you think he was scared? Why/why not?*

Christie Thomas

Day 4. Read Acts 9:22. *ASK: What was Saul telling people? Why was he telling people that? Have you ever told somebody that?*

Day 5. If you are able, spend a couple minutes on the computer before doing this devotion. Go to www.persecution.net and look at the "Persecution and Prayer Alert" for news about persecution of Christians in other countries. Find one that you feel is appropriate for your child, and use it to pray specifically.

SAY: Let's pray for people in _____ (country) *who are being hurt and put in jail by people who don't understand God's love.* Pray that they would be strong in the Lord, that people would come to know Jesus' love through their love, and that God would protect them from harm.

PRAYER:

Thank you, God, for protecting Saul from the people that wanted to hurt him. Help us to be bold in telling others about Jesus, just like Saul.

Amen.

Paul in a Shipwreck
Acts 27:13–28:10

Paul had been arrested in Jerusalem and was being sent to Rome to stand trial before Caesar. To get there, they had to take a boat, but they had quite an adventure on the sea! This week we'll be adventuring with Paul, hearing the whole story. After each reading, feel free to act it out with your child, have them draw a picture of the story, or just discuss it together.

Day 1. Read Acts 27:13–26. *SAY: Paul told them before they started sailing that they would have a shipwreck, but they didn't listen. Was he mad at them for not listening? How did he treat them? Let's ask God to help us treat people with respect even when they are rude to us.*

Day 2. Read Acts 27:27–38. *SAY: It sounds like all the sailors are very afraid. Why is Paul being so brave?* (In his letters, he explains that it comes from the grace he found in the Holy Spirit.) *How would you feel if you were in the middle of the ocean in a giant storm?*

Day 3. Read Acts 27:39–44. *SAY: In yesterday's story, Paul told the people on the ship that God had promised that no one would get hurt.* (Verse 34.) *Did God keep his promise? Isn't it amazing that God even protected the soldiers who wanted to kill Paul and the sailors who wanted to run away? God loves everyone and has a plan for each person's life.*

Day 4. Read Acts 28:1–6. *SAY: What is surprising about this story? The people from the island made a mistake in verse 6. Was Paul really a god?* (No!) *But God was taking care of him.*

Day 5. Read Acts 28:7–10. *SAY: The man's father was quite sick, but Paul healed him. How did Paul heal him?* (He prayed, the Holy Spirit helped him.)

PRAYER:

Thank you, God, for showing your awesome power to Paul and the sailors on the ship. Thank you for being a great and merciful God.

Amen.

Paul and Silas in Prison
Acts 16:16–36

Paul and his friend Silas helped a girl who was sick. But there were some people who didn't want her to get well; they got angry and made Paul and Silas get arrested. While they were in jail, Paul and Silas prayed and sang to God. Suddenly the walls and the floors started to shake, the chains fell off the prisoners, and the doors fell off their hinges! It was a giant earthquake! But even though the doors were open and their chains fell off, Paul and Silas didn't run away. Rather, they stayed behind to show Jesus' love to the jailer, who thought he'd be in big trouble if the prisoners had escaped. Instead he learned of God's great love for him, and his whole family chose to follow Jesus!

Day 1. Act out the story together. *SAY: What is your favourite part of the story?*

Day 2. Read Acts 16:23–36 from the Bible while your child draws a picture of chains.

Day 3. *SAY: While in jail, Paul and Silas did something strange. Instead of moaning and groaning, they prayed and sang. Why do you think they did that? Let's pretend that we're in jail right now, and we'll sing a song about Jesus together.*

Day 4. Sit on a bed or couch and pretend that you are in jail. *SAY: Here comes a big earthquake! The doors are open and the chains are off... what should we do? Uh-oh, here comes the man who put the chains on us. Should we beat him up and run away? If not, what should we do instead? What did Paul and Silas do?*

Day 5. *SAY: Peter and Silas had the chance to tell the jailer about Jesus. Read the part that says what they told him (Acts 16:29–33). Is this what our household believes? Have you been baptized like the jailer and his family?*

PRAYER:

Thank you, God, for showing your amazing power to Paul, Silas, and the jailer. You are big enough to cause an earthquake, yet you cared so much for each person in the jailer's family. Help us to love others like you.

Amen.

Loving and Listening to God

God wants our children to have a relationship with him, and building that relationship requires two-way communication. God speaks to us through his word, but he also speaks to us in other ways. In the Old Testament, we see God calling to the boy Samuel in the night and speaking to Elijah in a whisper. God rarely speaks in an audible voice like he did with Samuel and Elijah, but we can train ourselves to listen for his whisper in our hearts. When we know and love God, we can more easily identify his voice speaking to us.

Like it or not, God also speaks to our children through their parents. You have the great responsibility to:

> Impress [these commandments] on your children. Talk about them when you sit at home and when you walk along the road, when you lie down and when you get up. (Deuteronomy 6:7, NIV)

As you impress upon them the commands and stories of God, don't forget to teach them to communicate back to him, and to respond to him in love. As they respond to God by listening to him, serving others, praying, and worshiping, they will be building a relationship that will last for eternity. May your children truly become *wise for salvation*!

God Speaks to Us through the Bible

In the Bible, Jesus says, *"I will teach you the way you should go"* (Psalm 32:8, GNT). God has given us the Bible, which teaches us all about him. This week, we are going to go through a few of the most important lessons in the Bible!

Day 1. Read Genesis 1:1. *ASK: What do we learn about God from this verse? How powerful is God? How big is God?* (Major point: God is amazing.)

Day 2. Read Psalm 139:13–14. *ASK: What do we learn about God from this verse?* (Major point: God made me.)

Day 3. Read Zephaniah 3:17. *ASK: What do we learn about God from this verse?* (Major point: God loves me.)

Day 4. Read John 3:16. *ASK: What do we learn about God from this verse?* (Major point: Jesus wants to be my friend forever.)

Day 5. Read Matthew 22:37–39. *ASK: What does God teach us in this verse?* (Major point: What God wants of us in this life is to love him and to love others.)

PRAYER:

Thank you so much God for giving us the Bible. Help us to love to read your word, to think about it day and night, and to share it with others.

Amen.

God Speaks to Us through Our Parents

In the Bible, Jesus says, *"I will teach you the way you should go"* (Psalm 32:8, GNT). One of the ways that God teaches you is by giving you parents who teach you how to follow God. This week, we're going to look up some verses that talk about how God uses your parents to teach you about him.

Day 1. Read Exodus 20:12. *ASK: What do you think it means to honour your parents?*

Day 2. Read Deuteronomy 6:6–7. *ASK: When are we supposed to talk about God and the Bible? With whom are we supposed to talk about God?*

Day 3. Read 1 John 1:9. *ASK: Have you ever done something bad? Was I angry with you? Did I forgive you? When I forgave you, I was showing you what God is like. God doesn't like it when we do bad things, but he forgives us.*

Day 4. Read 1 John 3:1 (just the first sentence). *ASK: Close your eyes and imagine a cupcake. Now imagine that you are putting icing on your cupcake. How much are you putting on? Lots and lots, right? That's what the word "lavished" means. Just like we lavish lots of icing onto a cupcake, God has lavished so much love on us!* Now, let God's love flow through you as you have your child sit on your lap while you pretend to spread "love icing" on him/her. Have a good laugh, and revel in God's immense love!

Day 5. Read Ephesians 6:1. *ASK: Why are we supposed to obey our parents? Is that hard sometimes? Let's ask God to help us obey.*

PRAYER:

Thank you, God, for my parent(s). Thank you for giving them to me. Help my parent(s) to learn from you so that they can teach me about you.

Amen.

Loving God by Listening and Learning
Luke 10:38–42

Mary and Martha were two of Jesus' good friends, and they were sisters. One day, Martha was scurrying around, getting everything ready for Jesus, while Mary was sitting with Jesus and listening to him teach. Martha was really annoyed that Mary was just sitting there, so she complained to Jesus. But Jesus said something surprising to her; he said that it was even *more* important for them to listen to his words than it was to clean the house and cook food. So this week, we're going to practice loving God by listening to him.

Day 1. Read the paraphrase, then act out the story together. *ASK: Why do you think Jesus wanted Mary and Martha to listen to him?*

Day 2. *SAY: Practice turning on your listening ears, because it's time to listen to God! One way we can hear God is through the Bible.* Read Zephaniah 3:17 with your child. *ASK: What do you think God wants to say to us through this Bible verse?*

Day 3. Read the story directly from the Bible (Luke 10:38–42) or a children's Bible while your child draws a picture of a head with ears.

Day 4. Time to listen to God again! Read 1 John 4:19 with your child. *ASK: What do you think God wants to say to us through this Bible verse?*

Day 5. Today we're going to listen to God in a different way—if our hearts are open to him, God will often speak to us directly. Help your child get into a comfortable listening position, then pray the following prayer together. *SAY: Jesus, please help me to listen to you today. Help my heart and mind to be quiet so I can hear you. Jesus, what would you like to say to us today?* Once your child is ready, have them report back what Jesus said to them. Be prepared to be surprised!

PRAYER:

Thank you, God, for loving me. Please help me to learn to make my body be still and my thoughts quiet so that I can hear you speaking to me.

Amen.

Loving God by Serving
John 12:1–8

Jesus was visiting with Mary and Martha again, and while Jesus was sitting at the table, Mary took a bottle of very expensive perfume and poured it all over her feet. Then she wiped his feet with her hair. The others at the table thought this was totally crazy, but Jesus said that what she had done was beautiful. This week, we're going to practice loving God by serving him with our hands. Since Jesus isn't physically here to touch and serve, the Bible says that serving others will show that we love him.

Day 1. Read the paraphrase, then act out the story together.
ASK: Why do you think Mary poured the perfume on Jesus' feet?

Day 2. *SAY: We can show Jesus that we love him by serving each other. Let's think about a way that you and I can serve each other right now.* (Ideas: you could help each other get a drink of water, or you could help your child put pj's on, or your child could help you get your bed ready for bedtime. Let your child be creative!)

Day 3. Read the story directly from the Bible (John 12:1–3) or from a children's Bible while your child draws a picture of a fancy bottle of perfume.

Day 4. *SAY: The Bible says that the whole house was filled with the fragrance of perfume. What kind of things does our house smell like?* Together, see if you can find something that smells lovely—like a new bar of soap, a reed diffuser, or a bottle of vanilla. Talk about what it might be like to have your whole house smell like this because someone was covered in it.

Day 5. Using the sweet-smelling item from last night (or something different), plan to give it to someone as a way of serving them. Write a little note that says, "We can love Jesus by serving you" (or something to that effect). Plan to deliver it within the next twenty-four hours so you don't forget!

PRAYER:

Thank you, God, for loving me. Help me to show love to you by loving and serving other people!

Amen.

Loving God by Praying

Prayer is a very important way to show Jesus that we love him, because it requires talking to him and listening to him. Prayer helps us develop a relationship with God. We're going to try several different prayer activities this week. Use them in your future prayer times to help your child connect with God in the way that works best for him/her.

Day 1. Tactile prayer: grab a small ball or some rolled-up socks and toss it to each other. Every time you catch, say a prayer!

Day 2. Visual prayer: bring some pictures to prayer time with you. These could be pictures of family, a sponsor children, or almost anything. As you look at each picture, pray about it. For example, if it's a picture of your family, pray for your family. If it's a picture of a beautiful flower, thank God for doing such an amazing job of creating the flower!

Day 3. Auditory prayer: whisper/yell/use different voices during your prayers to God.

Day 4. Listening prayer: ask the following questions of God, then have your child listen for the answer and report back to you.

- God, will you show me something about you that I can say "WOW" about?
- Is there something I should say "sorry" for? Please forgive me.
- Can you please remind me of something that I can thank you for?
- Is there someone you want me to pray for?

Day 5. *SAY: There's another way we can love God with our mouths, and that is by using them to speak kind words to others instead of hurtful words. Can you think of a time when you said something that wasn't right?* Read Psalm 34:13 together. Try saying the verse out loud while holding your tongues! Talk about ways in which your child could use his/her mouth to love God.

PRAYER:

Thank you, God, for loving me! Help me to show you love by listening to you and talking to you. Help me to always use my mouth for good things, not for bad.

Amen.

Loving God by Worshipping

Worshipping God is one wonderful way we can show God that we love him, because in worship we are telling God how amazing he is.

Day 1. *SAY: One way to worship God is to tell him all the things that he's super good at. Let's think of some things that God is good at and tell him!* (For example, God is loving, and kind, and the smartest, and the strongest, and the most powerful…)

Day 2. *SAY: Another way to worship God is by singing songs to him and making music. Let's sing our favourite worship song together. (Or make one up!)* If you have children's instruments accessible, use them to have a little orchestra.

Day 3. *SAY: Another way to worship God is by reading out Bible verses that talk about how amazing God is.* Read Psalm 100 together with your child, repeating the words after you.

Day 4. *SAY: Another way to worship God with our bodies is to dance! Let's dance for God.* If you like, you can turn on some music, or sing a worship song while you dance together, or just let your child dance to the music in his/her head.

Day 5. You will need a piece of paper and a pencil. *SAY: One more way to worship God is to draw pictures of the things we love about him, or write those things down. Let's do that now.*

PRAYER:

Thank you, God, for loving me! You are the most amazing person in the whole wide world and I worship you.

Amen.

index

Christmas
- angel visits Mary...92
- Jesus is born...94
- shepherds...96
- wise men...99

Creation
- celestial bodies...9
- fish and birds...11
- Garden of Eden...17
- God rests...19
- land animals...13
- land, plants, and sea...7
- light and dark...3
- people...15
- sky and water...5

Daniel
- prays...85
- Shadrach, Meshach, and Abednego...87

David
- anointed...60
- cares for his sheep...63
- Goliath...65
- Jonathan...67

Easter
- Ascension...162
- Easter, short edition...152
- Easter, long edition...154
- great commission...160
- Palm Sunday...149
- road to Emmaus...158

Elijah
- and the widow...71
- fed by ravens...69
- listens to God...75
- Mount Carmel...73

Elisha
- and the widow...77
- Naaman...80

Esther...82

Gideon...50

God
- listening to and learning from...191
- praying to...195
- serving...193
- speaks to us through the Bible...187
- speaks to us through our parents...189
- worshipping...197

Jesus
- calls his disciples...111
- calming the storm...124
- caring for us...116
- catching fish for Peter...118

feeds the crowds...120
heals the blind man...135
heals the lame man...137
heals the ten lepers...139
how to pray...107
Lazarus...141
loving children...113
Mary and Martha...191
is annointed...193
obeys...103
two rules...105
walking on water...122
woman at the well...143
Zacchaeus...145
see also Easter, Parables

Jonah...89

Joseph
- the dreamer...25
- the forgiver...28

Joshua
- Jericho...48
- spies and Rahab...46

Moses
- birth...31
- the burning bush...33
- escape through the sea...37
- manna...41
- pillars of cloud and fire...39
- the plagues...35
- ten commandments...43

Noah
- ark...21
- flood...23

Parables
- good Samaritan...109
- great banquet...133
- lost sheep...127
- prodigal son...129
- prodigal son returns...131

Paul
- escape from Damascus...179
- and Silas in prison...183
- shipwreck...181

Pentecost...167

Peter
- catching fish...118
- escape from jail...177
- healings at the temple...172
- Tabitha...175

Ruth
- and Boaz...54
- and Naomi...52

Samuel
- and Hannah...56
- hears God...58

Timothy...170